Cambridge Elements ≡

Elements in Environmental Humanities
edited by
Louise Westling
University of Oregon
Serenella Iovino
University of North Carolina at Chapel Hill
Timo Maran
University of Tartu

BEYOND THE ANTHROPOLOGICAL DIFFERENCE

Matthew Calarco
California State University, Fullerton

CAMBRIDGE
UNIVERSITY PRESS

CAMBRIDGE
UNIVERSITY PRESS

University Printing House, Cambridge CB2 8BS, United Kingdom

One Liberty Plaza, 20th Floor, New York, NY 10006, USA

477 Williamstown Road, Port Melbourne, VIC 3207, Australia

314–321, 3rd Floor, Plot 3, Splendor Forum, Jasola District Centre,
New Delhi – 110025, India

79 Anson Road, #06–04/06, Singapore 079906

Cambridge University Press is part of the University of Cambridge.

It furthers the University's mission by disseminating knowledge in the pursuit of
education, learning, and research at the highest international levels of excellence.

www.cambridge.org
Information on this title: www.cambridge.org/9781108797375
DOI: 10.1017/9781108862769

First published 2020

A catalogue record for this publication is available from the British Library.

ISBN 978-1-108-79737-5 Paperback
ISSN 2632-3125 (online)
ISSN 2632-3117 (print)

Beyond the Anthropological Difference

Elements in Environmental Humanities

DOI: 10.1017/9781108862769
First published online: June 2020

Matthew Calarco
California State University, Fullerton
Author for correspondence: Matthew Calarco, mcalarco@fullerton.edu

Abstract: The aim of this Element is to provide a novel framework for gaining a critical grasp of the present situation concerning animals. It offers reflections on resisting the established order as well as suggestions on what forms alternative, pro-animal ways of life might take. The central argument of the book is that the search for an anthropological difference – that is, for a marker of human uniqueness determined by way of a sharp human/animal distinction – should be set aside. In place of this traditional way of differentiating human beings from animals, I sketch an alternative way of thinking and living in relation to animals based on indistinction, a concept that points toward the unexpected and profound ways in which human beings share in animal life, death, and potentiality. The implications of this approach are then examined in view of practical and theoretical discussions in the environmental humanities and related fields.

Keywords: anthropocentrism, anthropological difference, ethology, intersectionality, ontology

ISBNs: 9781108797375 (PB), 9781108862769 (OC)
ISSNs: 2632-3125 (online), 2632-3117 (print)

Contents

1 Introduction

The aim of this Element is to provide a framework for interpreting and gaining a critical grasp of the present situation concerning animals. In addition, it offers reflections on resisting the established order and suggestions on what forms alternative, pro-animal ways of life might take. Central to my argument is the idea that the search for an anthropological difference – that is, a marker of human uniqueness determined by way of a sharp human/animal distinction – should be set aside in favor of other ways of thinking about human-animal relations.[1] I suggest that the concern for establishing an anthropological difference, coupled with the establishment and maintenance of a series of practices, institutions, and ideologies aimed at giving higher rank to those deemed to be fully human, remains one of the key obstacles on the path toward a more just and more respectful way of living with animals and other nonhuman beings. In place of this approach, I sketch a different way of thinking and living based on what I call *indistinction*, a concept that points toward the unexpected and profound ways in which human beings share in animal life, death, and potentiality. I then examine this alternative mode of thought in the context of contemporary work on intersectionality, the environmental (post-)humanities, and related fields with a view toward establishing deeper connections between these fields and pro-animal research and activism. This work, then, is primarily written for and addressed to the following audiences: scholars and students who hope to gain a fuller sense of what is at stake in recent work in critical animal studies; advocates for social justice who wish to know more about how animal issues might figure in their work for the reconstitution of a society that eschews rhetorics and practices of dehumanization; and readers concerned with environmental justice and politics, who are seeking an alternative way of broaching the gap between animal advocacy and environmental issues.[2]

---

[1] A note on terminology: I use the phrase *human/animal distinction* (with a forward slash) to denote the traditional, binary manner of separating human beings from animals; I use the term *human-animal* (with a hyphen) to refer to similarities and differences among these beings that are nonbinary and relational. As just noted, the general aim of this book is to deepen the case for eschewing the traditional human/animal distinction and to create the space for alternative ways of thinking and living, a task that ultimately requires the invention of alternative concepts (besides "human" and "animal") that do justice to this richer vision. Like many authors who work on these issues, I desire to make use of another language for the beings under discussion, but the standardly proposed options (for example, the hybrid term *humanimal*, or writing the terms "human" and "animal" in quotation marks in order to indicate ironic usage, and so on) do not strike me as suitable. Consequently, I will use various combinations and reconfigurations of the terms human and animal throughout the book while acknowledging that they often fail to do the work I would like them to do.

[2] Readers who are somewhat new to these issues might find an earlier work of mine (Calarco [2015]) to be a helpful preface to this Element. For readers already familiar with that earlier work, the present project can be read as an attempt to fulfill a debt to correspondents and colleagues who

1.1 The Present Situation Concern Animals

The first task on the path that lies before us is to provide a forthright account of some rather dispiriting realities concerning animals within the current established order. Indeed, for those of us working in the fields of critical animal studies and animal activism, surveying the present state of animal welfare is a rather grim affair. As the daily news of atrocities in slaughterhouses, research labs, jungles, and oceans across the globe attests, violence against animals has been steadily increasing across multiple registers and domains for the past several decades. In just the past four decades, the number of land animals slaughtered for human consumption in the United States has increased from 3 billion to more than 9 billion (Jones and Pawlinger, 2017: 131, n. 148), while the annual global production of meat has more than tripled, from 100 million tons to over 300 million tons (FAO, 2014: 53).[3] At present, the global number of animals hunted and subjected to violent experimentation runs into the hundreds of millions on an annual basis,[4] and the number of animals killed by automobiles on roads and highways in the United States alone has been estimated at some million animals per day (Seiler and Helldin, 2006).

Animals are also suffering in ever-increasing numbers from the severe breakdown in the biophysical systems and habitats on which they rely. While climate change is already causing substantial deaths among certain animal species, increasing habitat fragmentation, soil degradation, freshwater scarcity, and other forms of ecological collapse are poised to accelerate this threat. A recent report notes that, since 1970, there has been a greater than 50 percent decline in vertebrate species populations due to these and similar causes (World Wildlife Fund, 2014).[5] While environmental scientists research the breaching of various "planetary boundaries" that threaten to undercut a "safe operating space for humanity" (Steffen et al., 2015), these same processes of degradation have already led to the deaths of countless individual animals and the extinction of numerous animal and plant species. Pro-animal activists and theorists are now facing serious questions about what animal liberation might mean when animals would be liberated into a world and a future in which the ecological

---

have asked for fuller discussion of the ideas on indistinction broached in the final chapter of that book.

[3] The Food and Agriculture Organization of the United Nations suggests that this number will increase to 455 tons by 2050. For more on this and related numbers, see Alexandratos and Bruinsma (2012).

[4] There is no single, agreed-upon source for these statistics, but all attempts I am aware of to track the number of animals hunted and subjected to invasive experiments on a global basis pin the number well into the hundreds of millions per annum.

[5] See van Dooren (2018) and Lorimer (2015) for informed discussions of the stakes and consequences of animal extinction from a perspective consonant with the argument developed here.

infrastructure on which they depend is no longer functioning sustainably (Best, 2014).

Just this small sampling of the stark realities of animal lives and deaths provides ample temptation to believe that mounting any serious resistance to the established order is essentially hopeless. Alongside these difficult facts, however, it must be noted that in recent years there have been important political successes concerning, and improvements in the lives of, animals. Just as we hear daily of atrocities committed against animals, we also hear of: animals being released from labs and given new lives in sanctuaries; friends, family, colleagues, and students becoming involved in pro-animal politics; and serious policy discussions concerning animal rights and welfare among the broader public. In brief, although the present is heavily tilted in the direction of increasing violence toward animals, there are growing numbers of individuals and organizations becoming passionately involved in contesting anti-animal violence and extinction.

It would not be inaccurate, then, to say that we find ourselves in the midst of what philosopher Jacques Derrida calls a "war ... over the matter of pity" (Derrida, 2008: 29).[6] He characterizes this war as a struggle between those who inflict violence on animals and deny responsibility for it and those who insist on compassion for animals and protest the violent nature of the status quo. Derrida notes that the war is unevenly divided at present in terms of the number and force of those who support either side. In relation to the hegemonic anthropocentric order, he suggests that those who defend compassion for animals have "minority, weak, marginal voices" (Derrida, 2008: 26). Yet, he is confident that, despite this current inequality in powers, the war over pity for animals is going through a critical transitional phase that will lead to fundamental changes and improvements in how animals are treated (Derrida and Roudinesco, 2004: 71, 73).

Whether such shifts toward increased compassion will in fact continue is something I will not speculate on here. What I do wish to underscore, though, is that struggles for animal justice are indeed passing through a critical phase, although I would characterize this phase in slightly different terms from those that Derrida uses. The crucial matter for us to understand is that even as pro-animal resistance is increasing, such advances in struggles for animal justice are being eclipsed by the rapid expansion of animal violence due to anthropocentric economic globalization and ecological breakdown.[7] Thus, the very nature of the

---

[6] For a thorough and penetrating account of this war from a distinctly biopolitical perspective, see Wadiwel (2015).

[7] Although I have here emphasized an increase in pro-animal politics among human beings, it is crucial to note that resistance from animals themselves constitutes another, often overlooked,

war over compassion and justice for animals is shifting underneath our feet. Now, more than ever, we need to take stock of our present situation, understand how we have arrived at this point, and begin to construct alternative forms of resistance to the dominant social and economic order.

1.2 A Guide for Readers

With this rapidly changing context in mind, the reflections presented in the pages that follow seek to reframe what is at stake in practicing pro-animal ethics and politics. The work proceeds with the hope that this reframing will afford a better sense of (1) how the established order is structured and (2) how productive linkages might be formed between and across movements dedicated to contesting (critically) injustice and constituting (affirmatively) more joyful and more beautiful ways of living.

The argument unfolds as follows. In Section 2, I offer an extended critical engagement with philosopher Hans-Johann Glock, who argues (contra the main thesis of the present work) for the importance of defining and maintaining an anthropological difference. This section will be of particular importance for readers who wish to understand the reasons for why many theorists in animal studies and the environmental humanities find the traditional human/animal division so questionable and why these limitations have generated the desire to develop an alternative way of thinking about human beings and animals. After arguing in Section 2 that the project of defining an anthropological difference should be set aside, I make the case in Section 3 for shifting the critical focus of pro-animal work away from *speciesism* (which can be defined as a form of ethical discrimination against animals based on the supposed superiority of the species *Homo sapiens*) to *anthropocentrism* (which can be defined as a set of institutions, systems, and practices that protect the existence and interests of a select group of beings deemed to be fully human). I contend that the concept of anthropocentrism better explains the manner in which (1) power and violence are directed at animals and more-than-human others and (2) normative consideration is often denied to marginalized groups of human beings. In Section 4, I explore possible relations between the critique of anthropocentrism and recent

---

aspect of this war. Attending to the chronological and ontological priority of animal resistance allows us to counter the well-meaning but problematic notion among some animal activists that human beings are fighting on behalf of animals who are somehow "voiceless" or without agency. The perspective developed in this book suggests that it is more useful to see this war as being fought among forces and powers that inhere in the fabric of life-death more generally and are not the sole provenance of human beings. Although it perhaps goes without saying, I should underscore the point that arguing for the priority and irreducibility of animal resistance is in no way intended to downplay or deny the radical structural and physical limits that are often placed on the agency of animals by anthropocentric institutions.

work on intersectional theory and practice. I suggest that if the analysis of anthropocentrism in Section 3 is roughly correct, this would imply that there are fundamental historical and material linkages between the kinds of violence directed at animals as well as human beings, linkages that make it possible to understand intersectionality in ways that go beyond the confines of intrahuman injustice.

In the second half of the analysis, beginning with Section 5, I move from a generally critical stance toward a more constructive and affirmative one aimed at developing alternative ontologies of human-animal relations and corresponding practices and forms of life. The term I use in this section for this alternative ontological perspective is *indistinction*, a concept that indicates the ways in which the traditional distinction between human and animal has collapsed, leaving the registers of human beings and animals in a profound state of indiscernibility. Section 6 continues the affirmative rethinking of pro-animal thought and practice as comprising three ethologies that function to reconstitute social, ecological, and mental relations with animals and a variety of earthly others. The final two sections examine the implications of the central critical and affirmative arguments of the argument. Section 7 explores the implied scope of the critique of anthropocentrism and the indistinction approach outlined in the previous sections. I argue here for an open-ended approach to ethics and politics, which includes human and animal justice struggles but simultaneously opens onto a variety of movements engaged with the more-than-human world. In Section 8, I broach the difficult question of how to navigate among the variety of ontological approaches and forms of life that are encountered in a non-anthropocentric context. While arguing for an affirmation of plural ontologies and forms of life, I also suggest that non-Western – and ongoing indigenous traditions in particular – offer crucial resources for reconfiguring relations with planetary kin of all sorts.

2 The Anthropological Difference

Animals have often been characterized as being radically different from human beings, as lacking some uniquely human traits such as reason, consciousness, language, or awareness of death. Further, this sharp difference has often been thought to entail that animals have lesser value and importance than human beings. This combination of a sharp human/animal distinction and value ranking is often referred to as a *binary* and *hierarchical* account of human and animal existence. It is a conceptual and normative pattern that occurs across many cultures and intellectual traditions but with striking frequency in the Western philosophical tradition in particular, from ancient Greece (Aristotle) and Hellenistic philosophy (Stoicism) to medieval (Augustine) and Renaissance philosophy (Aquinas), up through modernity (Descartes) and German Idealism (Kant and Hegel).[8]

Developing in tandem with this dominant philosophical discourse in the West, there has been a countertradition of minor, rogue philosophers and schools that offer more generous analyses of animal life and more complex conceptions of human-animal relations. That these kind of minor perspectives have had a persistent presence in Western philosophy should not be entirely surprising, for prior to the institution of ancient Greek philosophy, Homeric epic along with later tragic and comic poets (material that consistently served as a background reference for much of the philosophical work in ancient Greece) provided extraordinarily subtle reflections on the shared fate of human and animal life.[9] In addition, during the historical period in which ancient Greek philosophy was becoming an established practice and way of life, its primary thinkers and schools were in fairly regular conversation with non-Greek philosophical and mythical traditions that held more charitable and less anthropocentric ideas about animal life.[10] Thus, there have been a number of important figures throughout the history of the Western philosophical tradition, from antiquity to the present, including such philosophers as Diogenes the Cynic, Plutarch, Porphyry, Montaigne, Hume, and Nietzsche, who have challenged dominant accounts of the human/animal distinction, employing resources from this complex heritage. Very much like the "war over pity" that Derrida suggests is characteristic of our age, there has been an ongoing battle within the history of Western philosophy since its inception over how we should think about and interact with animals.

Unfortunately, in the standard narratives about Western conceptions of animal life offered by contemporary pro-animal philosophers and theorists, the importance and impact of most of these rogue figures are often overlooked in favor of an Enlightenment narrative in which Charles Darwin and evolutionary theory are seen as the sole forces that deliver the supposed death blow to reductive and binary accounts of animal life.[11] On the standard reading, evolutionary theory stresses the deep historical continuity among human life and other life forms and undercuts the idea of there being any kind of ontological rupture in these domains. Thus, rather than seeing a difference in kind between

---

[8] For a comprehensive critical survey of the Western philosophical tradition from this perspective, see Steiner (2005).

[9] Detailed accounts of, as well as primary source materials on, the status of animals in Greek antiquity can be found in Campbell (2014), Heath (2005), and Newmeyer (2010).

[10] A helpful exploration of these ancient cross-cultural connections is offered by McEvilley (2002).

[11] For a representative example of this approach, see Rachels (1991).

human and animal, evolutionary theory posits differences of degree, with more noticeable differences understood as emerging from shared building blocks. This scientific account of shared human and animal origins is depicted by many pro-animal philosophers as definitively replacing earlier dualist accounts of human and animal existence that were based on outmoded forms of Greek and Christian metaphysics. But this triumphalist narrative about the end of human exceptionalism due to the advent of evolutionary theory and the modern scientific worldview is more fantasy than reality. Consistent with the ongoing historical war just mentioned, there is still today consistent and considerable pushback on this conception of human-animal continuity, and not just from fundamentalist religious sources. A wide array of figures from philosophy in particular, and across the humanities and social sciences more generally, have continued to insist on the uniqueness of human beings over and against animals, despite overwhelming evidence to the contrary. Indeed, when one looks at the bulk of the work done in these fields today, it becomes clear that a commitment to the uniqueness of human nature remains not only operative but dominant. This trend can be seen with particular clarity in contemporary work done in the field of philosophical anthropology.

2.1 The Challenge of Doing Philosophical Anthropology Today

Philosophical anthropology takes as its charge the exploration of what constitutes human nature and human uniqueness. The general goal for researchers in this field is thus to determine an "anthropological difference" that sharply distinguishes human beings from other entities – and from other *animals* in particular, for it is along the human/animal axis that the most profound challenges to human uniqueness have been raised. Contemporary philosophical anthropologists are cognizant of the difficulties of establishing a strict anthropological difference, but it is to this task that they remain committed. What primarily motivates researchers in the field today is trying to reconstitute the grounds for the kind of work that is done in the humanities and the (human) social sciences. For, if there is no convincing way to distinguish human beings from animals, what would be the fate of those disciplines that are grounded on this distinction and its underlying commitment to human uniqueness?

   In order to explore the issues at stake here, it will be helpful to examine with some care a recent essay by philosopher Hans-Johann Glock (2012) entitled "The Anthropological Difference: What Can Philosophers Do to Identify the Differences between Human and Non-human Animals?" Glock's essay is significant in that it offers a forthright acknowledgement of the challenges contemporary researchers face in determining a uniquely human nature, noting that recent developments in evolutionary biology and cognitive ethology have led to a "general crisis in our self-image as human beings" (108). He acknowledges that nearly all of the traditional proposed candidates for the anthropological difference have been shown to be conceptually problematic or empirically false, either appearing in some form among certain animal species (or at least among particular individuals within a given animal species) or lacking in certain groups of human beings (or in particular individual human beings). Glock lists some twenty instances of claims to human uniqueness – from tool use to moral sense – that have all failed to establish an essential difference (111). That none of the traditional candidates for the anthropological difference have held up to critical scrutiny should not be surprising if we view the issue of human uniqueness from within a naturalistic, evolutionary perspective (as do most contemporary analytic philosophers). Ideally, the anthropological difference should delimit a capacity, characteristic, or behavior (or a set of such things) that is found in *all* members of the species *Homo sapiens* and *only* in members of that species. Such would be the kind of essential difference that marks human beings off from animals and that provides the necessary and sufficient conditions for group membership. But there is no reason to believe evolutionary processes will produce such clean demarcations between species. The variations found in and among species often make it difficult to identify any specific trait or set of traits that holds for all and only members of a given species. And even if such a rupture were to be identified, it would not indicate some timeless or essential difference between species but would simply mark the temporary and contingent result of an ongoing process of evolution (Hull, 1989: 11).

As Glock further concedes, it is of little help to move the search for an anthropological difference to the level of the genotype because the historical and current variation within the human species and the overlap with the genotypes of related species rule out any clean division (125).[12] Phenotypical differences (where markers of uniqueness have traditionally been sought) are no more promising as candidates, inasmuch as the variation among human beings at this level is enormous. No matter what specific trait, function, or behavior is

---

[12] This situation holds true even in those instances in which genes or microRNAs specific to the human genome are considered. It has been suggested in the popular press that FOXP2 or miR-941 are *the* markers of human difference, which is a deeply misleading claim. Not only do these specific genetic components *by themselves* mark no specific difference (how they are expressed and how they function in combination with other genetic components must be taken into account), but they are also sometimes deleted within given human individuals. For more on these issues, see Enard et al. (2002) and Hu et al. (2012). It should be noted that FOXP2 has been inserted into and studied in mice, using invasive methods; likewise, the presence and functioning of FOXP2 in songbirds and bats have been analyzed using invasive methods. In order to mark my strong disagreement with this kind of research, I do not cite it here.

proposed as the marker for human uniqueness, there will always be individual human beings without it; and if the characteristic or behavior chosen is so general as to be truly universal among *Homo sapiens*, it will almost certainly be found among one or more related species (126). Similarly, appeals to "potentiality" or "normality" will do nothing to resolve these problems within a naturalistic framework because variation within a species is neither accidental nor aberrational. Glock suggests that, at best, we might try to delimit a range of reaction norms that specify the range of possible developmental pathways for a given genotype in relation to different environments (126–27). However, given how wide this range is among human beings, such an approach would do little to help distinguish human beings from animals as such.

2.2 Anthropological Difference "Light" and the Social Turn

Readers who have been immersed in recent debates in philosophy of biology and animal ethics will be familiar with these and related problems concerning the establishment of an anthropological difference. Viewed collectively, they constitute a devastating attack on the very notion of human nature and rule out the possibility of establishing (at least on biological grounds) any traditional, essentialist version of an anthropological difference. Glock maintains, however, that an anthropological difference can still be maintained, albeit in a less ambitious form (he labels this less ambitious alternative *anthropological difference "light"* [128]). What needs to be acknowledged for philosophical anthropology to proceed, Glock argues, is that there is no version of an anthropological difference deriving from basic biological and naturalistic premises that can define a range of relevant capacities or traits found among all and only members of *Homo sapiens*. If we still wish to speak of human nature and the anthropological difference in view of these limitations, Glock maintains that we must shift the focus away from individual human beings and turn instead toward *social life* – that is, toward *species-typical behavior* in cultural settings.

It is important to pause here and note just how problematic this "social turn" (129) is. Glock's move away from individuals and toward species-typical behavior effectively means that in referring to an anthropological difference – that is, of a break between human beings and animals – there will be a significant number of individual members of the human species who do not fully match the definition of what is human. As such, it should be underscored that this approach to defining an anthropological difference is not actually interested in attending to the remarkable variation characteristic of the human species. It is instead focused on "the human," a partial and carefully delimited set of human beings that is believed to be cleanly and definitively separated from animals and other nonhuman beings. As one might suspect, there are problems and dangers with such an approach; indeed, the constraints at work in Glock's approach move uncannily in lockstep with the violent logic of the anthropological machine (as described by Giorgio Agamben), determining and fracturing the human along social-ontological lines and creating those divisions in view of a specific difference in relation to animals (Agamben, 2004: 29). Glock insists, though, that "there is nothing problematic about the idea that in contemporary circumstances humans typically develop in certain ways and hence have typical features and capacities" (128). Although one could imagine certain contexts in which such a statement might be true, it is most certainly *not* true in the context of debates about human nature and the anthropological difference. Few contexts, it could be reasonably argued, carry higher stakes.

Even with the adoption of this less ambitious notion of an anthropological difference based on the social turn and species-typical behavior, Glock admits that it remains difficult to locate a definitive human/animal difference. In order to do so, he notes we have to be able to answer the following two questions: "What features and capacities, if any, are present in all human societies and absent in animal societies? Which capacities are prerequisite for the functioning of human societies?" (129). To explain what is at issue in the second question, Glock offers the following troubling illustration: "no human society comprised exclusively of severe autists would be viable" (129). Such variations among human beings, then, will need to be set aside if we are to determine an anthropological difference based on the social turn. (That there are currently calls among autistic self-advocates of many sorts to have their communities recognized as cultures is not considered by Glock.) In regard to the first question, Glock has to tread an even finer line of inclusion and exclusion. As a first step, he argues it is necessary to focus only on extant societies among modern-day *Homo sapiens*; a broader historical approach, by contrast, would lead us into the rather problematic issue of how to separate *Homo sapiens* from extinct hominins, some of which likely shared with *Homo sapiens* nearly all of the social features and capacities that Glock has in mind. In addition, Glock acknowledges that even "viable" human cultures sometimes do not display certain features that are often claimed to be universal among human cultures. Here, Glock has to appeal to a modified notion of potentiality and suggest that these societies should still be seen as belonging on the side of the human inasmuch as they are *capable* of exhibiting all such typical features (his example is "cultural development") "given a suitable social context" (129). Conversely, behavior from animals who have been "enculturated" (i.e., trained to acquire specialized behaviors in scientific settings) can be safely ruled out of the discussion, Glock maintains, inasmuch as the behaviors exhibited in those settings do not form part of the normal developmental pathways of animals.

If we were to allow all of these caveats to govern the discussion, what kind of anthropological difference might emerge? For Glock, there is not one human/ animal difference that comes to the fore but rather a cluster of differentiating properties. He isolates the following behaviors and capacities as the best candidates for anthropological differences: a "special and highly complex" language; a "special and highly complex" form of sociality, which includes institutions and norms; and a "special" rational-technological plasticity that emerges from uniquely human cognitive abilities (130). With this cluster of properties in mind, Glock hopes to avoid the traditional requirement to determine a single anthropological difference (although if forced to do so, he notes that his "money would be on language" [130]) and move the discussion instead to the cluster of differences that can be found on the other side of the social turn.

2.3 Different "Epistemic Needs"

Of course, in adopting this kind of cluster approach, Glock's position will be open to objections of various sorts. His methodology is especially problematic because he cites no biological, sociological, or anthropological literature to support the notion that any of the distinctive behaviors or capacities he highlights are, in fact, entirely absent among all animals. A fuller discussion of that literature would no doubt force Glock to acknowledge that, even within the narrow set of constraints he advocates, the differences between human beings and all other animals remain primarily quantitative rather than qualitative. Given his evident familiarity with the ethological and comparative psychological literature, Glock is certainly aware that claims about some kind of special plasticity and sociality being absent in *all* animals are highly contentious.[13] Even the more "promising" claims concerning recursive language being absent in animals are by no means assured at present. Prior to laying out his three candidates for anthropological differences, Glock himself provides a qualifying claim on the issue of animal language (carefully couched in terms of "natural communication") in a footnote: "We may not know enough about the various channels of natural communication between cetaceans, in particular bottlenose dolphins, in order to decide how far they approximate linguistic communication" (129 n45). The same could be said, of course, about several other animal species.

Even if Glock were to concede these and similar objections, one gets the sense that such criticisms would fail to have any critical force for his project – because

---

[13] For helpful overviews of these ongoing debates, see de Waal (2016), Laland and Bennett (2009), and Lents (2016).

the idea of actually trying to attend to the complexity and variation of both human and animal life has long been left behind in his and most other discussions in philosophical anthropology. On the question of human uniqueness, we are to be enduringly committed – and *a priori*, as well, it would seem – to a distinction between the human and all other animals and to certain practices and forms of life that are built on that distinction.[14] If the distinction is troubled by some empirical finding or conceptual inconsistency, one can always move the goal-posts, change the constraints, redraw the lines, and get back to the task at hand, as Glock has done in view of previous scientific challenges.

Thus, rather than arguing point for point against Glock's premises as I have done up to this point, it might make more sense to examine what is actually driving this project of separating human beings from animals. Why does it matter in the final analysis whether we carry out this project? Clearly, the search for human uniqueness is not a neutral exercise in classification, so where do the ultimate stakes lie? For Glock, the stakes are to be found primarily in securing and maintaining the status and function of philosophical anthropology mentioned at the outset of our analysis. In defending the notion of an anthro-pological difference, Glock hopes to preserve philosophical anthropology as a specific philosophical approach in its own right as well as in relation to the grounding work it does for the human social sciences. Thus, the concern here is that, without *some* determination of human uniqueness, a great deal of philo-sophical and social scientific research will be undercut. This is a common worry among analytic philosophers who work on the topic of human nature and human/animal differences. For example, in a survey of recent research in this area, Maria Kronfeldner, Neil Roughley, and Georg Toepfer (2014) argue, like Glock, that the concept of human nature should be maintained against ongoing challenges. They suggest that human nature should be understood in a pluralistic manner, doing different work in different theoretical contexts depending on "our epistemic needs" (650). Inasmuch as "different scientific fields draw on different epistemic roles (definitional, descriptive, and explana-tory)" (650), they argue we will need to make use of different notions of the human and of several human nature*s*.

Such pragmatic concerns about maintaining the anthropocentric and excep-tionalist underpinnings of humanistic and social scientific inquiry are, from a certain perspective, entirely reasonable. After all, how can we expect to main-tain the disciplinary orientations of these fields without some notion of human nature that is relevant to their "epistemic needs"? If we lose hold of human

---

[14] Tom Tyler makes a similar point about an "uncritical prior belief in human uniqueness" that pervades theory and prefigures the human/animal distinction along certain anthropocentric channels (2009: 24).

uniqueness and have no way cleanly to differentiate human beings from animals (as well as other "others" of the human), what would become of the humanities and social sciences in particular? They would, of course, undergo a radical and thoroughgoing transformation. Perhaps, though, that is precisely what is needed. The current destabilization of the anthropological difference could lead to a complete rethinking of (1) how "the human" has been configured within these disciplines, and (2) how the disciplines might themselves be reconfigured in the face of these challenges. These are different "epistemic needs," to be sure, but which epistemic needs are most pressing is precisely what is at stake in this discussion. We are engaged here in a struggle over the future of thought, and it is not entirely obvious that traditional work in philosophical anthropology or the epistemic requirements of current research paradigms in the humanities and social sciences should be our sole guide in thinking about the anthropological difference.

Rosi Braidotti makes the important point that this kind of unmooring of the humanities and social sciences from their epistemological and anthropocentric foundations serves as a unique opportunity to create alternative lines of inquiry in the form of a "posthumanities" (2013: 145). This would not be a skeptical project content simply to undo the anthropological difference but would instead be aimed at pursuing a thought and practice of the human as being irreducibly caught up in and constituted by a series of more-than-human relations, networks, and contexts. According to Braidotti, the critique of anthropocentrism and human exceptionalism reconfigures the human so as to stress its "radical relationality, that is to say nonunitary identities and multiple allegiances" (144). She offers animal studies and ecocriticism as examples of the kinds of research programs and practices that have emerged from this post-anthropocentric approach. Supplementing Braidotti's point, I would suggest that this line of non-anthropocentric thought could be accelerated in order to reconfigure existing disciplines and also allow additional fields of thought to emerge through what she calls "humble experimentation" with the theoretical and practical implications of non-anthropocentrism (150). Important examples of such work are already unfolding in fields as diverse as anthropology, sociology, archaeology, geography, and political theory, where various "ontological turns" have served to bring more-than-human others of various kinds into the foreground.[15] These thought-provoking developments suggest that the destabilization of extant discourses that rely on a strong anthropological difference can generate novel research programs and need not lead to a reactionary retreat to anthropocentric terrain.

---

[15] For works representative of this trend, see Asdal, Druglitrö, and Hinchliffe (2017), Grusin (2015), and Wright (2017). I shall return to the ontological issues at stake here in the final section of the book.

3 From Speciesism to Anthropocentrism

Despite the promise of recent work on animals and animality (in fields such as human-animal studies, critical animal studies, anthrozoology, and so on) for this kind of critical transformation, it can be somewhat difficult to discern salient connections between animal-focused approaches and other trends within the posthumanities and environmental humanities. Indeed, pro-animal approaches have remained in many ways isolated from leading trends in the posthumanities and other critical theoretical and activist work. This isolation is doubly unfortunate, as (1) the insights of pro-animal work often fail to penetrate into other research in non-anthropocentric and critical political circles, and, conversely, (2) important trends within those fields often have very little impact on pro-animal work. In the next two sections, I propose a way of reconfiguring what is at stake in pro-animal discourse and activism in view of trying to address and overcome this limit. I suggest that one of the chief reasons for the relative isolation of pro-animal work is that it is premised on the idea that its main critical target is *speciesism*. I challenge this premise and suggest that, rather than focusing on speciesism, pro-animal discourse and activism should turn its critical attention toward *anthropocentrism*. It is anthropocentrism, I argue, that underpins the search for an anthropological difference over and against animals; and it is anthropocentrism that grounds not just violence toward animals but toward more-than-human others of many sorts as well as (paradoxically) certain groups of human beings. Thus, I suggest in this section that a critical focus on anthropocentrism (understood in a very specific sense to be articulated below) helps illuminate many of the problems with the established order, while also highlighting important conceptual and material connections between pro-animal approaches and related work addressing various kinds of injustices suffered by both human and more-than-human others.

3.1 The Problem with Speciesism

At present, there seems to be near unanimity among pro-animal theorists and activists that speciesism is the chief ethical and intellectual limitation that needs to be overcome in order to challenge the current status quo with regard to animals. Richard Ryder, who coined the term speciesism in 1970, defines it as "discrimination or exploitation" against a being from another species that is justified "solely on the grounds" of that being belonging to another species (Ryder, 1998: 320). As Ryder notes, "the speciesist regards the species difference itself as the all-important criterion" (320). Peter Singer, who is widely credited with popularizing the term, defines speciesism in line with Ryder as a "prejudice or attitude of bias in favor of the interests of members of one's own species and against those of members of other species" (Singer, 2002: 6). The chief problem with speciesism according to Ryder is that "species alone is not a valid criterion for cruel discrimination ... Species denotes some physical or other differences but in no way does it nullify the great similarity among all sentients ..." (Ryder, 1989: 6).

The concept of speciesism is often fleshed out by comparing it with sexism and racism, which are considered parallel and paradigm forms of selfish and unjustified discounting of the interests of others (Singer, 2002: 9). Thus, just as the racist or sexist discriminates against others on the basis of race or sexual difference, the speciesist discriminates on the basis of species differences. Such biological and physical differences (race, sex, species, and so on), it is argued by critics of these "-ism"s, are irrelevant to ethical consideration; as such, discrimination based on those grounds cannot be given cogent justification. Although various pro-animal authors define the term or expand on its meaning in slightly different ways, the basic definitions offered by Ryder and Singer as well as the parallels with racism and sexism recur throughout animal ethics and animal studies writings and pro-animal campaigns.

My intention here is not to diminish the important work that has been done around the concept of speciesism, for it has been enormously useful in helping to highlight some of the many ways in which animals have been discriminated against and subjected to harsh and unjustifiable violence. Along these lines, I am in fundamental agreement with pro-animal theorists who contest the established order's attempts to place animals outside the scope of normative consideration. I want to suggest here, however, that the concept of speciesism is perhaps not the most useful one for helping us gain a critical handle on the causes and nature of the marginalized status of animals in the dominant culture. Instead, I would argue that the concept of *anthropocentrism* is a more useful term for these purposes, and that it would behoove us to reorient animal ethics and animal studies away from a focus on speciesism and toward a critique of anthropocentrism.

In order to understand the stakes of this conceptual shift, it will be helpful first to consider some of the critical limitations inherent to the concept of speciesism. Common to much of the discourse surrounding speciesism is the idea that it is best understood as a prejudice, attitude, or moral deficiency held by *individuals*. To be sure, many individuals do in fact harbor negative attitudes toward animals that lead to their harmful or exploitative treatment. But is the widespread subjugation and violent treatment of animals best understood as the result of a series of individual actions and moral deficiencies? David Nibert compellingly argues that this individualistic understanding of speciesism betrays a confusion of ideology and system, or of prejudice and structure (Nibert, 2002: 7–11). If we are seeking to understand the foundations on which animal violence is established and reproduced throughout the dominant culture, it is more helpful, he suggests, to see our individual attitudes and prejudices not as the primary cause of the problem but as an ideological outgrowth of the institutional systems and economic structures that ground and frame our individual beliefs and actions. This kind of structural analysis does not deny individual agency, but it does shift the locus of where genuine power resides and of where efforts at transformation must be aimed. Individual attitudes and moral deficiencies undoubtedly need to be addressed, but they are not to be addressed simply through argumentation and education (which has most often been the dominant strategy of mainstream animal theorists, activists, and organizations); instead, bringing about fundamental changes in the basic structures and institutions through which we become speciesist individuals becomes a crucial point of concern.

Nibert's point gains additional force when we think about speciesism as a parallel phenomenon with sexism and racism. In light of recent social science research, few people would argue that sexism and racism are best understood as resulting from individual moral deficiencies. Moral shortcomings and intellectual inconsistencies certainly play some role in maintaining these stubborn problems, but we have come to view sexism and racism more fundamentally as systems of power, with deep historical, linguistic, institutional, and economic roots. As such, individual changes in moral attitudes, while vital, will not suffice to transform the larger structures and systems in which the institutional forms of racism and sexism reside. The same is no doubt true of the subjugated status of animals within the established order. The cultural and economic institutions through which violence toward animals is established and reproduced subtends and exceeds our lives as individuals, and our personal moral prejudices tend to grow out of and reflect these systems of power.

One of the effects of overemphasizing individual attitudes and prejudices in explaining the subjugated status of animals is that such an approach leads us to believe that the chief means for addressing injustices are also to be found at the individual level. In the standard philosophical narrative, individual prejudice concerning animals is supposed to be overcome chiefly through an engagement with the philosophical arguments concerning the supposed "irrationality" of speciesism.[16] As the standard narrative goes, finding oneself unable to refute the arguments that demonstrate the inconsistencies of the speciesist attitude, an individual finds herself moved by the force of reason to adopt an egalitarian animal ethic. From this non-speciesist intellectual foundation, she is then

---

[16] A version of this argument can be found in Singer (2009).

further moved to make the kinds of changes in her personal lifestyle that remove speciesist bias: for example, adopting a vegan diet, buying cruelty-free products, refraining from visiting zoos, and so on. The limitations of this individualist strategy become evident if we recognize that the deep structures and institutions that create the conditions for the subjugated status of animals remain largely untouched by changes in individual consumption patterns. Purchasing vegan food and cruelty-free products might send a less speciesist market signal, but such actions do not challenge the structural injustices of markets and the dominant socio-economic order, injustices that affect both animals and human beings in myriad ways.

If we continue this line of thought and turn our critical attention to an analysis of the dominant socio-economic structures that give rise to the violent exploitation of animals, we also notice straightaway that their logic is not "speciesist" in any significant way. The line demarcating those beings given full consideration by dominant institutions and practices has never tracked with the line demarcating biological species membership in *Homo sapiens*. There has *always* been unequal institutional standing among beings who are considered members of this biological group; and even the broadest and most generous "humanist" economic and legal frameworks continue to face intractable questions of what constitutes biological membership in the species *Homo sapiens* in view of beginning- and end-of-life markers, biological variations, hybrid species, and so on. In other words, the dominant culture and economy has never been and is not currently speciesist. As recent work on biopolitical approaches to animals has clearly demonstrated, what constitutes "the human" has always been subject to divisions and ruptures of various sorts that run within humanity itself; and the placing of animals and animality at varying points within and along this fragmented and divided terrain reflects less a kind of moral inconsistency and more the brutal lucidity of the machinations of sovereignty.[17] There are, of course, a handful of professional philosophers[18] who argue that ethical standing

---

[17] These points about biopolitical divisions internal to humanity are developed most notably by Agamben (2004), Esposito (2012), and Wolfe (2013), all of whom have been deeply influenced by Michel Foucault's seminal work on this topic.

[18] In his analysis of speciesism, Singer notes that in order to avoid it, "whatever criteria we choose [for inclusion within the moral community] . . ., we will have to admit that they do not follow precisely the boundary of our own species" (2002: 19). We should ask in response, though: How many people actually hold this kind of genuinely speciesist position that tracks precisely along the boundaries of biological species? Is this concept of an all-inclusive species membership notion of moral consideration actually the dominant logic of our main practices and institutions? It is true that at the rhetorical and conceptual level, some philosophers and theorists have been speciesist (and, a careful reading of Singer's early work shows that it is contemporary speciesist philosophers who are his primary targets along these lines); but here we are not simply trying to critique positions that a handful of professional philosophers hold. We are trying to comprehend and contest social and economic practices of power that have always given unequal and divided

should track perfectly along the lines of biological species membership, but this is a rather contemporary view and does not reflect the historical, hegemonic, and deep structural logic of the systems that lead to the subjugation of animals or other marginalized groups.

3.2 The Shift to Anthropocentrism

Thus, instead of focusing on speciesism, I would suggest that we think about the nature of violence toward animals and struggles for animal justice first and foremost through a critique of *anthropocentrism*. As the term is used here, anthropocentrism refers to a set of ideas, structures, and practices aimed at establishing and reproducing the privileged status of those who are deemed to be fully and quintessentially human. As just noted, in Western cultural and intellectual traditions in particular, the human (*ho anthrōpos*) has only rarely and recently been taken to denote human biological species membership; more commonly, the concept of the human comprises only a select group of privileged individuals. Among those select individuals, humanness is maintained by seeking to exclude or denigrate certain "animal" and "nonhuman" traits and behaviors considered to be both internal and external to humanness. What is included and excluded under the rubric of the human shifts over time, and group belonging expands and contracts depending on a number of factors. One theme that remains deeply consistent, however, is the importance that the relative inclusion and exclusion of animals and animality plays in relation to configuring the human. In my discussion of anthropocentrism here, rather than offering an exhaustive analysis of the concept, I focus primarily on those themes and features that help to highlight the relation between the human and animals/animality.[19]

Anthropocentrism is premised chiefly on the notion that the human is *exceptional* in relation to animals and all other beings. Characterized by purportedly unique and superior capacities and powers, the human justifiably becomes (on this account) the focus and center of attention. Thus, anthropocentrism is a kind of human narcissism, an attempt to grant importance, standing, and meaning to the human within nature and the cosmos as a whole. That there are certain points of continuity between human beings and animals has never been denied by the

---

status both to certain animals and certain groups of human beings in ways that do not track closely with the concept of biological species. The dynamics at work in this context are far more complex and are subject to continual modification and transformation; to understand and contest them requires a critical framework characterized by a corresponding flexibility and sensitivity to historical contingency.

[19] For broader overviews of anthropocentrism, see Crist (2018) and Steiner (2005). My analysis here is heavily influenced by Val Plumwood's (2002) reflections on anthropocentrism. I engage with her work at more length in Calarco (2014).

dominant intellectual and cultural sources of anthropocentrism. But what allows human exceptionalism and narcissism to be established and maintained is, as we have seen, the claim to a specific *anthropological difference*. Thus, even though humans share certain behaviors and characteristics with animals, anthropocentric logic posits that there must at some point be a sharp ontological rupture along certain axes wherein the human in its unique form emerges. Often, this rupture is attributed to capacities such as mind or language, or sometimes to a cluster of emergent traits (as is the case with Glock's approach), that grant human beings their unique mode of existence.

This kind of exceptionalist ontology forms the deep background against which our normative, legal, and economic systems function. With the uniqueness of the human taken for granted, the circle of consideration is drawn tightly in line with the contours of the human and its interests. Full consideration need not be given to all human beings within an anthropocentric context, as not all human beings necessarily carry the unique traits of the human. Likewise, granting full or partial consideration to beings or species that are biologically nonhuman does little to disrupt the basic logic of anthropocentrism if that extension is based on such entities being similar to, or being in the best interests of, paradigm members of the class of the human. Typically, however, anthropocentric logic reserves full consideration for only a fraction of humanity; and even the most progressive anthropocentric humanisms do not usually argue for consideration and standing to extend to *all* members and instantiations of *Homo sapiens* (despite lofty rhetoric to the contrary). At an institutional level, the lack of any ethical standing for nonhuman beings leads in our age to most animals and more-than-human entities being reduced to property under the law and to commodities within the economy. Laws are designed with the interests of the human in mind, and markets are created and maintained to further the economic interests of the human alone.

So, what is to be gained if we take the concept of anthropocentrism as our critical point of departure? First, this concept better accounts for the subjugated status of animals as well as marginalized groups of human beings. The systems of power and control that structure modern societies are unevenly distributed among both human and animal populations, a fact that is easily overlooked if we think that speciesism is the main problem at hand. If we examine the established order looking for speciesist forms of discrimination, we would expect to find individual ethical prejudices that operate according to a strict human species/ nonhuman species division. But what we find instead are ideologies and institutions that grant full standing and privilege only to certain groups of human beings while excluding large swaths of humanity and the vast majority of animals and more-than-human others from consideration.

In addition, an analysis of anthropocentrism helps us better understand why certain animals are elevated over other animals and even over other (often marginalized) human beings. Typically, the animals that receive privileged or protected status in anthropocentric societies are given that status for reasons germane to the interests of those deemed fully human (e.g., pets might at certain times receive elevated status insofar as they matter to human beings with full standing). Likewise, with the handful of animals for which full legal rights are sought (typically, mammals who display higher-order cognitive abilities and subjectivity), a certain strain of anthropocentrism is often still at work in such instances. Such animals will only gain full legal standing by way of exhibiting strongly analogous or identical traits or capacities with the human. Other animals, along with certain human individuals and groups, who fall too far outside the scope of the dominant subject position of the human are fated to various sites either on the edges, or entirely outside, of the community of protected beings. It is precisely in view of such exclusions and marginalizations that great care needs to be exercised in regard to the adoption of strategies for seeking rights for animals, inasmuch as the criteria used to bring animals within the orbit of the established order will undoubtedly be found only among a small handful of animals; such criteria will likely also be used to justify excluding certain human beings and much of the more-than-human world from full protection.

At the normative level, a critical analysis of anthropocentrism allows us to rethink what is at stake with the question of moral consideration. Critics of speciesism have often taken for granted that our current normative theories are sufficient for our interactions with other animals, as long as we are consistent with the basic premises of those theories and avoid excluding animals simply because they do not belong to the human species. Whether we endorse consequentialist, deontological, virtue ethical, contractarian, or any of the other major normative theories, philosophers have sought to show that these theories need not exclude other animals from consideration in principle. That such frameworks tend to exclude some human beings and rather large numbers of animals from consideration has not necessarily been a fatal objection for most critics of speciesism, as the aim of much of pro-animal ethics has been rigorously to avoid species-based discrimination rather than to develop a broadly-inclusive framework. A thoroughgoing critique of anthropocentrism should make us skeptical of this standard approach to animal ethics. The foregoing analysis would suggest that this sort of approach – which draws lines of consideration around select groups of human beings and animals –constitutes yet another iteration of anthropocentrism, with traditional human traits and capacities still occupying the center of ethical attention. A genuine challenge to anthropocentrism requires a rather different normative approach, one that displaces "the human" from the central locus of concern and that rethinks human-animal relations from the ground up. In Sections 5 and 6, I will propose one way of assuming this task. Before doing so, I turn in Section 4 to the issue of how a critique of anthropocentrism might help us to reframe the stakes of pro-animal politics and form more fecund connections among a variety of radical struggles for justice.

4 Anthropocentrism and Intersectionality

Another upshot of turning our critical analysis away from speciesism and toward anthropocentrism is that it helps to illuminate how the multiple lines of power and oppression that structure human culture intersect with and co-constitute many forms of human-animal interactions. As a number of scholars have demonstrated, discriminatory practices aimed at human beings – such as racism, colonialism, sexism, ableism, and so on – tend to bleed into the dominant culture's relationship to animals.[20] Animals suffer under (and, on rare occasions, benefit from) extensions and iterations of the structures of de- and sub-humanization aimed at human beings; hence, it is essential to appreciate that a stand-alone speciesism cannot fully explain the status of animals within the established order. Conversely, the analysis of how violence and power circulate through and among animal bodies is crucial for understanding what is often considered to be exclusively intrahuman violence. A wide variety of disciplinary apparatuses, technologies of control, and institutional logics of inclusion and exclusion have originated in human-animal relations; and it is rare that such modes of violence and sovereignty remain limited to the orbit of human-animal relations.[21] In general, anthropocentrism – as a logic, as a set of rhythms and habits that structure everyday life, and as a set of institutions and practices aimed at securing the privileged status of those deemed to be fully human – operates on and among bodies and lives of all sorts and does not respect species boundaries.

What the foregoing analysis suggests, then, is that the various modes of oppression and structures of violence and power that have formed the critical focus for much of the work of human social justice struggles are themselves instances of anthropocentrism. Much as is the case with dominant forms of human-animal interactions, social injustices often pass through and are caught up in anthropocentric logics that are predicated on human/animal and human/nonhuman

---

[20] For representative examples of such work, see Kim (2015), Singh (2018), Adams (2015), and Taylor (2017).

[21] Fuller discussions of the interpenetration and co-constitution of apparatuses of violence directed at human beings and animals can be found in Derrida (2008), Pugliese (2013), and Wadiwel (2015).

distinctions; and the same holds true, conversely, for trying to understand many of the injustices suffered by beings in the animal and more-than-human world. This is why it is essential to view anthropocentrism, rather than speciesism, as one of the primary sites of the critical focus for struggles for animal justice and social justice. Let me emphasize that I am *not* arguing that radical social justice struggles are themselves simply instances of anthropo-centrism; rather, I am suggesting that struggles against social injustice should also be conceived as struggles against anthropocentrism (understood in the broad sense discussed above) and hence as allied (but not reducible) to other movements against anthropocentrism. Although mainstream versions of social justice struggles do sometimes uncritically repeat anthropocentric logics and norms, the more radical and militant strains of these movements have long recognized that the marginalized and dispossessed are seen by the dominant order as not fully human; further, these more radical movements have emphasized that justice is to be achieved not by acceding to the privi-leged position of "the human" at the expense of other marginalized beings but rather by taking leave of this kind of hierarchical social order in favor of creating one that is genuinely universal. Such radical, non-anthropocentric trends are found within nearly every major struggle for social justice, and they form fecund and crucial points of contact for building bridges between human, environmental, and animal politics.[22]

At issue here is the deepening of analyses and strategies of resistance that render manifest the interconnected and interlocking systems of power that cut across the human, animal, and more-than-human worlds. What must eventually become axiomatic is the idea that if we are seeking to contest and transform power structures that encompass and control both human and nonhuman forms of life, then contestation of these structures that remains focused strictly on the intrahuman register is an insufficient strategy. An approach that remains limited to an intrahuman focus allows anthropocentric logics and practices to spread uncontested to other nonhuman domains, with the inevitable consequence that these forms of anthropocentrism will rebound on marginalized human lives and communities. Likewise, the notion that animal activists can focus solely on what is "good for animals" while ignoring anthropocentrism and social injustice in other registers has to be seen as being equally limited and problematic in perspective and strategy. As just noted, anthropocentrism operates on human and nonhuman registers in differential, interlocking, and self-reinforcing ways. Thus, to focus solely on discrimination against animals and leave other modes of discrimination unaddressed (or, worse, to assume that they have already been

---

[22] For thoughtful explorations of these themes, see Kim (2015) and Pellow (2014).

essentially eliminated) is to commit a grave error that undermines struggles for both human and more-than-human justice.

Many pro-animal activists and theorists have previously caught sight of these interlocking connections and intersections. But because the concept of speciesism has been the guiding thread through which the connections were made with other forms of discrimination, the approach to building solidarity with other struggles was often based on an attempt to show that violence toward animals was the result of the same kinds of "irrational prejudice" that supposedly gave rise to sexism, racism, classism, and so on. Further, in order to make a compelling argument for animal liberation within the context of other justice struggles, significant efforts were made to analogize and even strictly equate violence directed toward slaves and marginalized human beings and violence directed toward animals (often referred to as "dreaded comparisons").[23] Clearly, this strategy has not led to the desired results of creating lasting linkages between animal liberation and human social justice movements and has instead tended to generate a backlash from the latter movements.

It might be tempting to see this backlash as an instance of obstinate anti-animal bias, but I would suggest other dynamics are at play here. The attempt to show that violence toward animals is analogous or equivalent to racism, sexism, classism and other forms of oppression can be carried out in a variety of ways. When (as has often been the case) such connections are drawn by theorists, activists, and organizations within the animal liberation movement that are not seen as having demonstrated genuine solidarity with social justice struggles, the efforts tend to ring hollow. Also, if the equivalences and analogies are drawn in a quick, unthinking, or insensitive manner, they also tend to be rejected by those who struggle for social justice.[24] Ultimately, it must be acknowledged that large numbers of mainstream pro-animal theorists, activists, and organizations have often been entirely absent from the most pressing social justice and economic movements of our age. If, however, the broader pro-animal movement comes to be seen as fundamentally committed to radical social justice struggles, both in word and deed, the responses from activists across the spectrum would undoubtedly be far more positive and supportive. I am not implying that such commitments from animal liberationists would lead to an immediate outpouring of support for pro-animal causes or uniform solidarity in all instances. Anthropocentrism and violence toward animals contaminate the entire culture's thoughts and practices in countless, subtle ways that can be hard both to identify

---

[23] Marjorie Spiegel (1996) offered the original version of this "dreaded comparison" approach to linking speciesism to various forms of intrahuman discrimination. For an excellent discussion of the positive potentials and critical limitations of dreaded comparison analyses, see Socha (2013).

[24] Boisseron (2018) provides a particularly incisive analysis of the dynamics at play in this context.

and overcome. As such, even the most radical and critical struggles for human social justice can sometimes reproduce certain anthropocentric logics and practices. But overcoming such limitations becomes far more likely if pro-animal causes are seen as being in genuine solidarity with those movements from which they seek support.

I should emphasize that what I have just written about placing solidarity with social justice movements more in the foreground of animal justice struggles should not be taken to suggest that the issues of violence and control over animal lives are somehow secondary to dealing with human injustice. Pro-animal activists and theorists are certainly correct to insist that animals have suffered tremendously under the reign of anthropocentrism; and even in those limited cases where animals have received privileged or protected standing within the established order, those positions have come at the cost of animals being subject to sovereign control in other problematic ways. Thus, to show strong solidarity with human social justice movements does not require giving up on pro-animal politics or making such work secondary in importance to any other cause; what *is* required, and what will make animal liberation and animal justice movements grow in force and numbers, is to ensure this work is driven by a steadfast commitment to ending anthropocentric injustices in their many, interrelated forms.

Indeed, if the foregoing analysis of anthropocentrism is correct, struggles for animal justice must if anything become *more* visible on the political scene, insofar as work that is done to break down hierarchical and violent human/animal divisions is exceedingly important for disclosing some of the more subtle and stubborn machinations of intrahuman anthropocentrism. By carefully examining the lives of beings (like many animals) who have been determined by definition and kind to belong permanently outside the orbit of the human, we gain a much clearer picture of the inner logic and proble-matic underside of discourses and practices aimed at protecting the privilege of the human. Thought and practice that proceeds from within these critical spaces helps to undermine claims that the anthropocentric order can some-how be expanded or reformed to do justice to those who have traditionally been placed on its margins. Anthropocentric institutions and practices con-tinually produce violent zones of inclusion and exclusion – borders, thresh-olds, and outsides – that serve to shore up the sovereignty of the human. From this perspective, the point of genuine justice struggles – whether they are undertaken in view of marginalized human beings or other beings who have been deemed sub- or nonhuman – should be to contest the anthropo-centric order of things and to create radically non-athropocentric forms of life.

This sort of broad non-anthropocentric project can best be understood as an extension of extant forms of theoretical and political activity. Perhaps the strongest and most fruitful example of such work can be found among pro-animal feminists and ecofeminists more generally.[25] What is particularly significant about the work carried out under these headings is that it is deeply intersectional in terms of its critique of power, simultaneously working with multiple critical perspectives. On the feminist side of this project, there exists a long history of feminist politics and theory that has emerged through serious engagements with a wide variety of other social justice movements. Feminists today generally accept the notion that the critique of sexism must, for contingent historical reasons and as a matter of political solidarity, involve a critique of a whole host of other forms of oppression; this is due in large part to the indefatigable work of women of color feminists who have made a powerful case for the irreducible necessity to think and act critically in intersectional terms.[26] This rich, intersectional vision of social justice has been subsequently expanded by ecofeminists and pro-animal feminists to include a consideration of the ways in which the logics and practices of social injustice are also at work in relations with animals and the nonhuman world more generally. In brief, using the terms developed above, ecofeminism and pro-animal feminism are calling attention to the ways in which anthropocentrism creates caesuras and fractures internal to the human as well as in relation to what is understood to be nonhuman. These theorists and activists urge us to understand anthropocentrism and its effects on human and more-than-human beings as the result of an interlocking, overlapping set of power relations – relations that must be jointly critiqued and resisted.

Ecofeminism and pro-animal feminism have had mixed fortunes on the theoretical and political scene in recent years, with their influence going into decline for some time but currently making a comeback in social justice and environmental justice movements, and in recent work in new materialist feminism, animal studies, and pro-animal activism. Although I think we should strive to maintain the particular configuration and conjunction of feminist, animal, and ecological frames, I am not advocating remaining locked into this specific approach. Rather, I would suggest that the aim should be both to maintain ecofeminist/pro-animal feminist analyses while expanding that

---

[25] Rather than trying to canvass this enormous literature here, I point the reader to two key sources: (1) Donovan and Adams (1996), a classic collection of essays on the intersection of pro-animal and feminist politics; and (2) Adams and Gruen (2014), an anthology that comprises a wide variety of pro-animal and ecofeminist perspectives that have emerged in recent years.

[26] This literature is too vast to cover here. For readers looking for a helpful overview, see Collins and Bilge (2016).

kind of intersectional approach toward other, somewhat neglected move-ments. We are currently seeing the formative stages of this kind of work in the expansion of critical animal studies (which builds on an already well-established anarchist and Critical Theoretical intersectional analysis and alliance politics) as well as in efforts to bridge pro-animal theory and activism with movements that have not seen much attention among animal liberation-ists, such as critical race theory, critical disability studies, and indigenous decolonial struggles.[27] These intersectional projects represent just a handful of the important efforts that are currently being undertaken by theorists and activists to help animal liberation and animal justice struggles mature into broad, powerful movements that offer an important critique of the dominant social order while also developing forms of life beyond anthropocentrism.

4.1 A Coda on Intersectionality and Animals

As promising and insightful as such intersectional work might be, it also has certain limits in terms of its explanatory reach and political effectiveness. It is commonly understood that intersectional analyses allow for the relative auton-omy of each region of analysis (race, class, gender, and so on) and aim to avoid the kind of reductionism in which one form of power (say, gender) might be explained away by another (say, class). If this kind of autonomy is borne firmly in mind, then it would be equally important to note that the exploitation of animals must be understood as having its own specificity and importance, independent of any contingent linkages with human injustice. Thus, the exploi-tation of animals should be seen as an important issue in its own right and should not become a point of concern only insofar as it happens to be linked to one or another form of human social injustice (Clark 2012).

Similarly, there are limitations with an intersectional approach in regard to animals to the extent that intersectional thinking was originally developed to understand the formation of marginalized human subjectivities inside human social institutions. While one of the key lessons of animal intersectionality theorists has been that such vectors of intra-human power relations bleed into the animal world, it is not altogether clear that the capture and confinement of animals has been done primarily with the aim of forming animals (or other nonhuman beings) into subjects with disciplinary identities. Power works in various ways and toward various ends; and to understand how it circulates through and among what are called "animals" might require different analytical

---

[27] For a small sampling of this work, see Boisseron (2018), Chen (2012), Harper (2010), Nocella, Bentley, and Duncan (2012), and Robinson (2013). I briefly return to these themes in the final section of the book.

approaches that focus specifically on the techniques applied to such beings and that attend to alternative kinds of social formations.[28] None of this is to suggest, of course, that we should simply do away with intersectional frameworks; rather, the point here is to acknowledge the *relative* autonomy of animal issues and to recognize that incommensurabilities between intersecting struggles will no doubt arise. Indeed, one of the most important tasks of intersectional and radical politics today is the ongoing work of trying to find ways of helping these critical tensions to become productively incorporated within those struggles that aim to build livable futures.

5 Indistinction

In the previous sections, I have argued for the following points:

1. The traditional search for an anthropological difference is no longer a tenable project for a variety of empirical, ontological, and normative reasons. Not only does a focus on human exceptionalism create the conditions for violence toward animals, but it also provides support for the dehumanization and subhumanization of beings deemed to be lacking in full humanity (Section 2).
2. The "logic," or patterns of thought, at work in the quest for an anthropological difference and in the mistreatment of animals are better understood as a form of anthropocentrism rather than speciesism (Section 3).
3. A critical analysis of anthropocentrism helps to illuminate important linkages and points of commonality among struggles for animal justice and related struggles for human and more-than-human justice (Section 4).

Up to this point, my argument has been largely critical and diagnostic in nature, dedicated to the task of trying to discern the deep anthropocentric logic and structures that give rise to intolerable forms of violence directed primarily at animals but also at marginalized human beings and more-than-human others of various sorts. In the remainder of this discussion, I move from a critical to an affirmative mode, starting with a fresh look at the ontology of human-animal relations and then offering some reflections on how pro-animal discourse and practice might be transformed once the quest for an anthropological difference is left behind.

Let us assume, then, that we accept that anthropocentrism and the traditional quest for an anthropological difference are problematic ways of thinking and living. Such an assumption would entail, first of all, setting aside the project of determining what distinguishes human beings from animals. But if we set aside

---

[28] This point is persuasively made by Stanescu (2013) in the context of biopolitics and by Puar (2011) in the context of feminist theory.

the human/animal distinction, the first question that comes to the fore concerns its replacement. What (if any) ontological and normative coordinates should guide our thinking about human beings and animals if we no longer have this traditional distinction to guide us? A considerable amount of work in the fields of animal studies and the environmental humanities is dedicated to thinking carefully about this question, and at present there is no consensus regarding a single replacement framework. Rather, there are several general approaches that have been adopted and that are in the process of being elaborated. At this point, I want to explain and recommend a general way of thinking about human-animal relations that I refer to as the *indistinction* approach.[29] One way to illuminate some of the key features and merits of the indistinction perspective is first to contrast it with another way of thinking that has recently become dominant in animal studies, an approach that emphasizes human and animal *differences*. Let us begin with a very brief discussion of the central idea of the difference approach and then turn to a fuller elaboration of the indistinction approach.

5.1 The Difference(s) Approach

The difference (or differenc*es*, in the plural) approach begins from the premise that classical human/animal binary oppositions of the sort that we have critically analyzed in previous sections are clearly untenable and must be replaced with more refined sorts of distinctions. Of chief importance to this approach is the recognition that binary oppositions tend to reduce the ontological richness of both sets under consideration. Thus, with regard to the human/animal distinction, if we begin from the assumption that there must be a single line of division between human and animal, we will tend to emphasize the factors that make a given set homogeneous and overlook the internal richness and multiplicity of that set. We will also be disposed to miss the complex differences that we might find between those sets – which is to say, there need not be a single difference (as with classical binary logic) or a single set of differences (as with Glock's more contemporary approach) that differentiate human beings from animals. Instead, given the sheer size and complexity of the sets under consideration, we should expect to encounter complex differences of various sorts along this boundary. The difference approach, then, does not so much aim to eliminate the distinction between human beings and animals but instead presents distinctions and differences in more complex and refined terms. Jacques Derrida, who is perhaps the

---

[29] Although I refer here to indistinction as a single approach, as will become clear in my analysis, it is informed by several ontological and normative frameworks. The implications of such ontological and normative pluralism are addressed in Sections 7 and 8.

most influential representative of this differences-based perspective, argues that our goal should be to *complicate* and *multiply* human/animal differences so as to affirm the richness and multiplicity of both sets and the complexity of the ontological, existential, and historical relations between human beings and animals (Derrida, 2008).

One of the merits of the difference approach is that it does not tie normative consideration to identity – in other words, animals and other beings are not taken into consideration within this framework based chiefly on how much they are "like us." Where classical versions of the human/animal distinction employ sharp divisions to justify ethical rankings the difference approach instead multiplies divisions between and among human beings and animals and thereby removes the foundations for any definitive value ranking based on a clear and simple ontological division. In principle, this gesture allows the scope of consideration to be understood in extraordinarily broad – perhaps unlimited – terms.[30]

There is, however, a lingering problem that haunts the difference approach, at least as it is developed in the work of Derrida and those who adhere closely to his variant of deconstruction. The problem concerns precisely how human/animal differences are conceived and affirmed. For difference-based thinkers, as we have just noted, the classical approach to distinguishing human beings and animals is overly reductive and simplistic and should thus be jettisoned for a more careful and refined account. Yet, this critique of the traditional human/animal distinction is undertaken not in view of eliminating that distinction or downplaying its significance. Rather, the difference approach proceeds under the assumption that there is something worth preserving in this opposition and that it marks off some salient feature regarding ontological and normative matters. Thus, even if none of the traditional markers of human propriety suffice clearly to demarcate human from animal, the difference approach does not suggest that we should altogether abandon discussions about anthropological differences.

It is worth pausing, however, to consider whether this strategy is a cogent one. If, in fact, the project of determining differences along a human/animal axis faces intractable difficulties, what reason is there for insisting on refining and complicating this opposition? Would it not be more sensible simply to hold that opposition in abeyance and turn theoretical and practical attention in other directions? After all, not all distinctions are worth preserving, even those with venerable pedigrees like that of the human/animal distinction. And if we do

---

[30] Not all theorists inspired by Derrida share this expansive view of the ethical. See Wolfe (2013) for an argument for why ethical relations should be attributed only to properly *responsive* human and animal beings.

insist on refining this distinction, do we not constantly run the risk of re-focusing attention on human propriety at the expense of other questions, concerns, and responsibilities? On questions such as these, difference theorists (foremost among them, Derrida himself) have offered precious little in the way of explanation or justification. Instead, this approach seems to have been adopted largely out of a failure of imagination regarding other possibilities.[31]

5.2 Human-Animal Indistinction

The approach I will develop from here onward, an approach governed by what I am calling a logic of *indistinction*, has a great deal in common with the difference perspective as just articulated. However, the indistinction approach sees the destabilization of the human/animal distinction as being much more thoroughgoing and having far more revisionary implications than does the difference approach. Indeed, the term *indistinction* points toward the way in which the collapse of the tradition human/animal distinction is taken to be complete and irreparable.[32] As we have seen, this division purports to mark some sort of definitive and salient difference between the set of human beings and all nonhuman animals. If *human* and *animal* are understood as they are commonly used in standard philosophical and biological registers, then the task at hand in deploying the human/animal distinction would be tantamount to trying to discern a rupture between some 7.7 billion human beings on the one hand and countless billions of animal species and individuals on the other. Even if we were to limit the analysis to extant species and individuals (and thereby set aside the complicated question of whether *Homo sapiens* can be clearly differentiated from extinct hominin species), intellectual honesty forces us to acknowledge that we lack anything even approaching full knowledge of either the human or animal worlds. With regard to beings typically classified as animals in particular, we have only *identified* a small fraction of the planet's animal species, let alone lived with them for any length of time or tried to enter into their life-worlds.

---

[31] My remarks here about the difference(s) approach and Derrida's work have been deliberately brief, intended as they are to serve as a way of understanding the stakes of adopting the perspective of indistinction. Those readers who defend a difference-based approach will no doubt wish to see a more extensive and more charitable engagement with this approach before considering alternatives. I have attempted to provide such an engagement in various places; see especially Calarco (2008) and (2015).

[32] Within the context of animal studies, the most important figure for opening the door to a thought and practice of indistinction of this sort is Donna Haraway (2003, 2008). Although I disagree with many of the positions Haraway takes in regard to transforming human-animal relations, I have benefitted greatly from her insights on negotiating the human/animal distinction. I engage with her work at more length in Calarco (2015) and in a forthcoming monograph on the place of animals in the history of philosophy.

In view of the sheer richness of the sets under consideration, the project of trying to discern whether animals do or do not share in what are taken to be character-istically human capacities or traits would seem to constitute a quintessential instance of what Nietzsche calls the "*hyperbolic naiveté*" of anthropocentrism (1967: 14). To avoid such naiveté, we might humbly consider setting aside the search for an anthropological difference. If we no longer insist that the human serve as the measure for ontological standing, value, or significance, then the questions of whether human beings are unique or whether animals are "like us" recede into the background. This gesture of abeyance allows us, in turn, to adopt a different posture – one that places human beings squarely among animals and other planetary and cosmic kin. From this less arrogant perspective, we can begin to catch sight of the myriad ways in which "we" might be and become "like them."

5.3 Shared Conditions

What would it be like to acknowledge that we are indiscernible from animals and animality, with no exceptions or qualifications, and without any nostalgia for securing an anthropological difference? If we were to assume this posture, we would enter into an ontological register where there is no assured propriety and where traditional logics of identity and difference are no longer functional. Philosophy and "theory" more generally would be returned to the space in which they are perennially called and provoked into existence, namely, the site of wonder. In this domain, the fitting response to ontological indiscernibility is not anxiety over securing one's propriety and identity but joy in the face of exploring and experimenting with what Brian Massumi (2014) calls *mutual inclusion*: that is, shared conditions, overlapping experiences, and common fates. In assuming this disposition, we encounter the kind of surprising and disavowed intersections with animal life and death from which the established order has long sought to distinguish itself: not just shared vulnerability, finitude, and mortality, but also the mixed and messy passions and possibilities of bodily and earthly immanence.

Consider just a handful of examples of this kind of affirmative disposition toward and recognition of human-animal indistinction:

1. Virgil expresses such a perspective in the *Georgics* when he ruminates on the manner in which erotic passions overtake and animate all earthly species:

   > Every last species on earth, man and beast alike, the vast schools of the sea, the cattle and bright-colored birds fall helpless into passion's fire: love is the same for all. (1963: 242–44)

2. The author of Ecclesiastes (traditionally referred to as Qoheleth) under-scores the joint fate of human beings and animals in their shared mortality,

an unavoidable condition that threatens to dissolve the significance attributed to the purportedly exceptional nature of human existence:

> I said in my heart with regard to human beings that God is testing them to show that they are but animals. For the fate of humans and the fate of animals is the same; as one dies, so dies the other. They all have the same breath, and humans have no advantage over the animals; for all is vanity. All go to one place; all are from the dust, and all turn to dust again. Who knows whether the human spirit goes upward and the spirit of animals goes downward to the earth? (*Ecclesiastes* 3: 18–21, NRSV)

3. Margaret Robinson (Mi'kmaq) describes how animals might be seen if approached not as a separate class of distinct entities but as kin, as beings who belong on a continuum with other human beings, as a member of "all my relations" (*M'sit No'kmaq*). As a child, Robinson grew up by a lake near a wooded area and developed a particular fondness for frogs. She recounts a story of her father rushing into the house one day after a powerful rainstorm, asking her and her siblings for help. A frog had laid a number of eggs in a puddle and the puddle was drying out, putting the eggs at risk of dying. Her father told them they needed to get the eggs into the pond as soon as possible to make sure they didn't die. As Robinson explains:

> For the next two hours, in the hot sun, we moved these gelatinous frog eggs and these squirmy little tadpoles from a shrinking puddle into the pond, from the puddle to the pond, from the puddle to the pond, again and again. And as we did so, I realized that, to my dad, the fragility of these animals mattered in the same way that our own fragility mattered. So, for me that was concrete experience of what "all my relations" actually means. It means let me not forget our mutual vulnerability, and let the way that we treat one another reflect the kinship ties that bind us all. (Robinson, 2014)

Such perspectives on and experiences of indistinction refer not so much to common *powers* over which we have control but to shared *conditions* into which we fall, into which we are thrown, side by side with animals and the more-than-human world. And if we bear these profoundly shared, indistinct conditions firmly in mind, it reinforces a kind of ontological and normative humility. We gradually lose interest in thinking about what constitutes anthropological distinctiveness and turn instead to recognizing and affirming that we participate in a world that precedes and exceeds us in every temporal and spatial direction.

From a perspective of indistinction, animals and more-than-human Others of various sorts are also seen as beings from whom we might learn how to live – indeed, from whom we might learn how to live *well*. We find this kind of affirmative attitude toward animals, for example, in the ancient Cynics, who were notorious for turning their backs on the philosophical project of establishing human propriety.[33] The Cynics believed that it was a mistake to sequester ourselves in a city-state and govern ourselves by norms and laws meant to ensure a human way of life separate from animals and nonhuman nature. Cynics sought instead to live according to and alongside nature (*kata physin*), affirming the indistinct zone that conjoins human with animal life and arguing that genuine flourishing is to be found in that shared site. The Cynics went so far as to make nonhuman animals *exemplars* of the good life, modeling their day-to-day lives on the remarkably simple and reliably contented ways in which many animals live. The ancient historian Aelian relates the following tale of Diogenes the Cynic that illustrates this sort of zoomimicry aimed at flourishing:

> Diogenes was bereft of all company and left all alone. He neither received anyone, because he was so poor, nor did other people invite him into their houses, because he put them off by his accusatory manner and the way in which he disapproved of all that they said and did. So Diogenes was thoroughly dejected and was eating barley-bread and leaf-tips, this being all that he had at hand. A mouse came along and fed on the crumbs that dropped from his hand; and as Diogenes watched it busy at work, he smiled and became more cheerful and contented, saying, "This mouse has no need of any of the luxuries of the Athenians, and yet you, Diogenes, are downcast because you are not dining with the Athenians." And so he achieved contentment of mind when it was most needed. (Aelian, 1997: 13.26)

For those of us who have been formed within a culture dedicated to human propriety and separation from animals and nature, the ideal of living according to nature – of living like an animal, in the sense that Diogenes catches sight of here – is something that must be *accomplished*. As Michel Foucault notes, animality of this sort is achieved only through training and practice (*askēsis*) (Foucault, 2011: 265). Living like an animal is not simply a matter of rejecting the dominant culture in favor of some set of supposedly primal animal impulses and instincts, but instead entails the development of a third nature that overcomes the de-formative aspects of the second nature acquired from the dominant anthropocentric culture in which many of us are immersed from birth. The perspective of indistinction thus provides a kind of portal through which such an *askēsis* (and the specific strategies and rituals for accomplishing it) might be glimpsed, a project to which we will turn in the following section.

---

[33] According to legend, Plato was once giving a lecture at his Academy on human nature and defined human beings as "featherless bipeds." Diogenes is reported to have interrupted the lecture by running into the Academy holding a plucked chicken and announcing: "Here is Plato's man!" (Diogenes Laertius, 2018: 279 [6.40])

It should be noted that the emphasis the logic of indistinction places on shared and overlapping conditions does not preclude the recognition of salient differences and various types of singularity. Indeed, the argument being offered here is that acceding to and assuming an optic of indistinction is the *precondition* for a thought of radical alterity. If thought and life remain tethered to and organized around an anthropological difference – or even around its expansion (as with traditional animal ethics) or its complication and refinement (as with deconstructive approaches to animal studies) – then myriad differences that unfold along other axes continue to go overlooked. Thinking about human beings and animals in terms of indistinction allows us to set aside a rather clunky opposition (human/animal) in order to explore and experiment with other ways of seeing, thinking, and living. On this approach, refined forms of difference and different kinds of singularities begin to emerge in places where we might have least expected them, preparing us to recognize contaminations, becomings, and mutations that have occurred and continue to occur through and across human beings and animals and that undo reductive conceptual designations.

6 From Ethics to Ethology

In the previous Section, I sketched in the contours of the concept of indistinction, focusing primarily on its general ontological dimensions and underlying affective dispositions. As a means of filling in this broad sketch, I turn in this Section to an examination of some of the practices and forms of life that align with indistinction. In particular, I am interested in exploring what would typically be called an "ethics" of indistinction, although I want to suggest that the term ethics needs to undergo revision, expansion, and reorientation when brought into contact with the logic of indistinction. The specific practices I analyze here are perhaps best understood as a series of experiments with alternative modes of relation and ways of living, although variants of such experiments have long been undertaken by certain minoritarian individuals and groups. I describe these practices as "experiments," then, not out of any desire to avoid an explicit commitment to a particular tradition or to established rituals and practices. Rather, it is the historical and lived contexts in which we find ourselves that require continual innovation and experimentation.

As noted in the introduction, we exist in the midst of widespread ecological upheaval (which includes, but goes well beyond, climate change), along with widespread migrations (that are related, but not limited, to economic transformations) and increasing encounters among and between human and more-than-human species on an ever more crowded planet; what is more, all of these shifts are taking place against the backdrop of an established social order (in both its

conservative and progressive manifestations) that is neither willing nor pre-
pared to come fully to grips with these and related changes. In view of such
conditions, the practices discussed here can perhaps best be understood as
preparatory, even incubatory – providing sites for breeding experimental practices and dispositions that might be of more general use if and when more
favorable conditions emerge. I should also note that the specific themes and
practices emphasized here are not to be taken as exhaustive of what a thought of
indistinction might entail, nor are they meant to exclude other visions, traditions, or forms of life. Rather, the vision proposed here is speculative, open-
ended, and suggestive. It is based on a long-term immersion in and interaction
with various theoretical and activist communities dedicated to rethinking
human-animal relations and should be seen as indebted to and speaking in
support of such efforts at living worthwhile lives in the context of rapidly
changing planetary conditions.

6.1 The Three Ethologies

When pursuing a thought of indistinction, the initial challenge is to reverse the
flow of our ethical reflections in order to develop a more humble disposition,
one in which we see ourselves as relative latecomers on the evolutionary and
historical scene, plain members and citizens of a world that is exceedingly
abundant in animal and more-than-human lives and relations.[34] As recently
arrived guests, we might see our ethical task as learning how to inhabit these
longstanding, ongoing more-than-human worlds and ways of life in a manner
that is more respectful and that adds to their existing richness and beauty. In order
to be good guests of this sort in regard to animals in particular, we would need to
achieve a more refined understanding of their worlds and of the possibilities for
developing hospitable relations with them. To take up such a project would thus
mean that animal *ethics* would become one aspect of a broader set of *ethologies*.

Ethology is commonly invoked in discussions of animal ethics – especially
when ethologists provide scientific evidence of animal behavior that debunks
traditional claims about animals lacking a specific trait or capacity that has been
used to exclude them from the scope of ethical concern. But the notion of
ethology I have in mind here is much broader than just the scientific analysis of
animal behavior and is intended to be put to a much more complex set of ends.[35]

---

[34] I am here echoing language from Leopold (1989: 204). See also Hudson (2015: 230).

[35] The ideas outlined here are inspired variously by Félix Guatarri's "three ecologies" (2000),
Gilles Deleuze's (1988) and Vinciane Despret's (2016) thoughts on philosophical ethology, as
well as the practices and writings of a number of radical ethologists and philosophers such as
Jane Goodall, Barbara Smuts, Marc Bekoff, and Dominique Lestel. I offer a fuller account of the
ideas presented here in a forthcoming project on deep ethology.

I understand the term ethology to comprise three different but related registers: *social*, *environmental*, and *mental*. All three of these registers are at work in the Greek word *ēthos* (ἦθος), from which ethology derives. The term *ēthos* can be used to mean custom, in the sense of the shared practices and relations that constitute a given social order; thus, we could speak of a *social* ethology that is aimed at a careful study and consideration of what constitutes social life among animals as well as between human beings and animals. In many ancient Greek sources, *ēthos* is also used to refer to the typical haunts or dwelling places of animals and human beings; thus, we could refer to an *environmental* ethology that undertakes an analysis of human-animal relations within their environmental milieu. In ethical contexts, *ēthos* (sometimes modified to ἔθος with an epsilon, *ethos*) is often understood as referring to the habituated dispositions and formed character of an individual; along these lines, we could consider the development of a *mental* ethology that investigates the various practices that form and re-form the character and subjective constitution of an individual animal, whether human or more-than-human.

If we understood our ethical task as etho-logical in these multiple senses, we might then turn from the standard project of revising or extending extant normative frameworks and instead undertake the work of fundamentally transforming our individual, social, and environmental worlds. Elsewhere, I have discussed in some detail what such transformations might look like using the example of radical ethologist Joe Hutto's work with mule deer (Calarco, 2018); here I will simply highlight some salient details that will help us gain a better sense of what practicing indistinction might entail. Hutto's project, which he chronicled in a book (2014a) and documentary film (2014b), took the form of a seven-year-long immersion in a herd of mule deer, animals who generally avoid contact with human beings. Hutto's idea for immersing himself in the life of a particular herd of mule deer was given to him by the mule deer themselves, some of whom seemed to be interested in approaching him and his partner both for food and companionship. With incredible persistence and patience, Hutto gradually went from spending short periods of time on the periphery of the deer herd to becoming a fully acknowledged member of it, with the deer eating directly from his hands, affectionately rubbing their bodies against his on their own initiative, exchanging information with him through bodily signs, and sharing their joys, sorrows, and daily lives with him.

Hutto's written and cinematic reflections on this long-term ethological project make it clear that his relations with the mule deer brought about a complete conversion along all of the registers outlined above. His sense of what constituted his *social* life and who his kin were was utterly transformed as he came to be accepted as a full member of the mule deer herd rather than being seen simply as an outsider studying them from afar. Similarly, Hutto came to gain a profound understanding of the importance of the natural *environment* in the lives of the deer pack – not simply in the sense that the deer had a subtle and complex relation with their ecology but also in the sense that ecological degradation of various forms (from habitat destruction to climate change) made the already-difficult lives of these deer additionally precarious. Hutto's *mental* life and subjectivity also underwent a complete transformation. His sense of who he was as an individual changed as he found himself being recurrently touched and shaped by deer perspectives, interests, and passions. Ultimately, Hutto's experiences with the mule deer gave rise to a vision of the good life that placed seeing and living in the world through and alongside others at its core.

I highlight Hutto's project here not to suggest that each of us should undertake these kinds of long-term, radical ethological experiments. Rather, the point is to think about how we might enact and undergo variants of such ethological transformations in our own lives, communities, and contexts. For example, a significant number of readers of this present discussion likely find themselves in urban settings, surrounded by various species of birds and perhaps other animals such as squirrels, rabbits, coyotes, skunks, raccoons, and possums. What if these animals were no longer seen as part of the background of our lives but as full members of a larger *socius* of which we ourselves are plain members? If we came to attend to these animals on a regular basis – perhaps by ensuring they have adequate water and food, or by observing them carefully and at length, or by simply engaging in daily rituals that recall us to their singular presence and lives – might we not then begin to give more careful consideration to how our way of life impacts theirs? How do our daily modes of eating, purchasing products, transportation, working, and so on positively and negatively impact animal life? And how might we transform our ways of life to ensure that they and we are able to flourish jointly? We might further wonder: What kinds of individuals would we have to become to be worthy of such relationships? What kinds of subjective transformations might we have to undergo in order to live lives that do justice to this larger sense of community?[36]

The underlying assumption enabling and guiding this kind of deep ethological work is that human beings and animals are indistinct – which is to say, that there is no clear-cut ontological difference that bars the possibility of experiments in plasticity with various species. We cannot know in advance what else we – or the animals with which we undergo such experiments in living and knowing – might become; such realities can only be determined in and through

---

[36] See Wolch (1998) for a profoundly insightful set of reflections on renewing human-animal relations along these lines.

the experiments themselves. Practicing ethics as ethology is aimed at creating relations that render alternative ways of life possible with and alongside earthly others. Such practices are guided by an acute awareness of the need to go beyond minor changes in patterns of individual consumption or incremental structural reforms. By respectfully and thoughtfully immersing ourselves in the life worlds of other individual animals and various animal assemblages, we are able to gain a fuller sense of the kinds of changes needed to enable joint flourishing in the context of a world undergoing rapid and radical change. At present there are dozens of remarkable projects and initiatives that have been proposed along these lines, including: building refuges for animals, alter-wilding habitats, de-paving our roads and systems of transport, experimenting with ecological architectures, and so on. But such projects will remain largely abstract ideals unless they emerge from the sorts of ethological experiments in living differently under discussion here. At bottom, it is not so much a matter of pitting structural changes against individual subjective transformation (as the standard debates among activists would have it), but rather of appreciating the need to have large-scale structural changes driven by impassioned subjects who have an *existential* stake in ensuring they are actually brought to fruition.

7 Beyond Animals?

The present work is appearing in the Environmental Humanities series of Elements, in which related volumes will examine themes ranging from the more-than-human environment to landscapes to objects and beyond. As such, it will be useful to consider the role that reflections on animals play in this broader environmental context. The previous generation of philosophical work on ani-mals, which was carried out primarily in the context of analytic animal ethics, was often pitted in an antagonistic way against the broader concerns of the fields of environmental ethics and environmental studies. Whereas environmental theorists focused on ecosystems, life in general, bioregions, landscapes, and so on, animal ethicists tended to limit their analyses to individual animals who were characterized by one or more ethical traits or capacities (sentience, subjectivity, agency, and so on) that resembled human beings in some ethically salient way. While animal ethicists sometimes accused environmentalists of being fascistic holists and undermining the ethical standing of individual moral agents and patients, the reverse charge was often aimed at animal ethicists who, it was argued, failed to move beyond atomistic and individualistic ethical frameworks to consider the interests of broader, more-than-human communities.

My hope is that the logic of indistinction and critique of anthropocentrism I have developed above will provide a different way of thinking about the relation of current work in animal studies to emerging research in the environmental humanities. In line with the argument regarding the posthumanities presented in Section 2.3, I want to suggest that the conclusions defended there make it unnecessary to draw any sharp break between work dedicated to thinking about animals and projects aimed at other aspects of the human and more-than-human worlds. The first point to bear in mind on this issue is that the critique of anthropocentrism proposed in Section 4 should make us wary of thinking that, in staking out a site beyond the anthropological difference, we have arrived at a place where anthropocentric dogmas are somehow held fully in abeyance. The anthropocentric image of thought that many of us have inherited encourages us to give primary distinction, rank, and value to those who are considered full members of the kind *anthrōpos*. The most common way of contesting this logic in pro-animal circles is to insist that the scope of *anthrōpos* has been unfairly delimited, and that certain groups of human and more-than-human beings are carriers of whatever markers of propriety are supposed to be exclusive to that select subset of humanity. I have argued that this critical gesture, however important and strategically necessary it might be in certain instances, tends to deepen anthropocentrism – albeit under a new, more expansive guise.

I have further argued that the overarching goal of the critique of anthropocentrism should not be to expand its logic or make it empirically consistent with its own claims; rather, the goal should be to displace "the human" in a fundamental and radical manner from the center of ontological and normative reflection. To think and live in a radically non-anthropocentric way thus entails letting go of our traditional concern with what constitutes human uniqueness and instead allowing thought and life to be animated by other passions and interests. It also demands letting go of "the human" as a measure of value and as the anchor for ethical life; for "the human" has served not only as an ontological point of orientation but also as a referent for demarcating the boundaries of where ethical obligations begin and end. Within the dominant anthropocentric logic, if I can know who is fully and properly human, I can then determine where my ethical obligations begin and end. In this way, anthropocentrism brings the question of ethical consideration to a standstill and allows normative thought to achieve a sort of dogmatic closure. But if we no longer know what a human being is, and are no longer sure of what delimits human from animal or human from more-than-human, then anthropocentric ethics loses its foundation and driving impetus. To own up to human and more-than-human indistinction of this sort means turning away, without nostalgia, from the project of determining propriety and the boundaries of ethical life, and instead redirecting our attention toward the human and more-than-human worlds as sites for ethico-ethological experiments in living well. Here the human is stripped of its traditional role of being *pantōn chrēmatōn metron* (the measure of all things), and value, meaning, and existence are seen to emerge in and through experiments with relations and beings that exceed the boundaries of the human.

This kind of non-anthropocentric approach would seem, however, to have no limit in terms of the beings, systems, and relations with which/whom experiments in living differently might occur. Who can predict in advance what kinds of values and meanings might emerge in such relations – or the beings, sets, and assemblages through whom these things might be constituted? To be sure, the kinds of ambiguous and complex ontological and normative reconfigurations we have examined at the human/animal border are not limited to that particular site. So, let us assume that a non-anthropocentric way of life takes this kind of open-ended form and that there can be no *a priori* means for knowing where ethico-ethological relations might lead. Under this assumption, two lines of questioning arise: (1) If ethico-ethological life is, in fact, open-ended in this way, why has the focus of this Element has been primarily on animals? Is there any justification for this restriction in focus? (2) Even if there is no *a priori* justification for limiting ethics to a particular species or set of beings, is it not essential to provide our normative reflections with *some* center, anchor, or guidepost in terms of who does and does not count?

Following Jacques Derrida, I would suggest that "the question of the animal" ought not be reduced to or eliminated by another question or analytic framework. Questions concerning animals and the human/animal distinction are important in their own right and also carry important strategic value (Derrida and Roudinesco, 2004: 62–63). In terms of the latter issue of strategy, as I hope to have demonstrated in the preceding discussion, the examination of issues surrounding animals is crucial insofar as it helps to illuminate the inner workings of anthropocentric logic in a variety of contexts – which is to say, questions concerning animals are not only relevant to animals. How the human is conceived and how numerous modes of "othering," dehumanization, and subhumanization are carried out are brought into greater relief when examined specifically in relation to animals and animality. It is now becoming increasingly clear that the standard sociological categories that ground critical theories (such as race, class, gender, sexuality, and so on) cannot be separated from the rhetorics and practices that surround animality and animals themselves. There is, of course, no *essential* linkage between the marginalization and dehumanization of human beings and the othering logics to which animals are subjected; the linkages posited here are entirely historical and contingent in nature, and at some point in the future, consideration of such connections might become less salient. But, for the purposes of gaining a critical understanding of the history of the present established order, the question concerning animals remains fundamental.

In addition to the strategic value of a focus on animals and animality, the approach outlined in this Element is motivated by the intrinsic importance of issues surrounding animal life and the fate and existence of animals themselves. The critical analysis of anthropocentrism and the sketch of the logic of indistinction I have offered are aimed at understanding, on the one hand, some of the key sources of the violence directed at animals and, on the other hand, the rudiments of other ways of conceiving human-animal relations that allow for more respectful, creative, and beautiful modes of living and dying with them. To be sure, the ideas suggested here will not apply to every being we might consider an "animal" (whether that term is used colloquially or in a strict biological sense); nor do they imply any commitment to the maintenance of that particular concept of "animal". Rather, the path of thought pursued here proceeds in view of what are *called* "animals," in both colloquial and biological terms – and in view of what those beings, relations, and assemblages might otherwise become, beyond the boundaries of the anthropocentric categories and institutions that currently shape their lives and deaths.

My insistence on the intrinsic and strategic importance of the question of the animal should not, however, be read as endorsing a normative zoocentrism. The critique of anthropocentrism I have defended entails both the simultaneous displacement of *anthrōpos* from the center of ethics and the refusal of the notion that ethics has a center. Animal and environmental ethics has been plagued by never-ending debates on what should constitute the primary locus of ethical consideration, with candidates ranging from human beings and animals to ecosystems and living beings in general. Some recent work in the environmental humanities risks falling into this same pattern of trying to discern *the* essential critical and affirmative center for theory and practice, whether it be animals, plants, species extinction, or an intersectional assemblage of one sort or another. We should be highly skeptical of this tendency to find a new anchor or center for ethical consideration, as it mirrors the deep structural logic of anthropocentrism in reverse. The most effective way to displace anthropocentrism and to avoid reconstituting its pernicious logic is to reject altogether any final determination of an ethical center. No set of entities or relations, no territory or region need occupy the permanent center of normative consideration, reflection, or practice. Rather, various registers of concern will to come to the fore as they become salient in specific theoretical and practical contexts, and ebb to the background when they become less salient. Further, it is essential always to bear in mind that the more-than-human world places its own demands on thought and life and retains the persistent potential to call into question whatever normative schemas might be deemed central or final.

8 Ontologies and Forms of Life

Alongside these questions about the scope and structure of normativity beyond the anthropological difference, we are confronted at the end of our reflections with questions about the ontological commitments underlying this project. The general aim of this project has been to argue that standard iterations of the human/animal distinction – especially those aimed at trying to establish and maintain a specific and stable anthropological difference – are no longer tenable. But recognizing and affirming that critical limit does not, by itself, provide any clear indications or pathways for how a non-anthropocentric mode of thought might be developed. In the second half of the discussion, I have made certain suggestions about how thought might proceed in a post-anthropocentric context, especially in regard to the ontological aspects of human-animal relations that highlight the mutual indistinction of human and animal.

I use the term *suggestions* here advisedly, as the perspectives and related practices I have elaborated under the rubric of indistinction should be seen as experimental, provisional, and speculative in nature. The need for intellectual caution and humility on this terrain cannot be underestimated, for it is all too easy to reinstitute anthropocentric modes of thought, given that anthropocentrism of one sort or another has been the dominant ideology for millennia in the traditions in which many of us live and think. Likewise, it is essential to guard against the kind of reactionary gesture that almost always accompanies the dissolution of dominant intellectual coordinates. Anthropocentrism and its logic of human exceptionalism have traditionally been presented as an exclusive worldview and way of life; and anthropocentric practices and institutions have been established historically through a wide range of violent intellectual and material practices that have sought to annihilate alternative visions and ways of life. Thus, when anthropocentrism and the quest for human uniqueness are set aside, we cannot help but feel that something has been lost, that our orientation for thought and practice has gone missing. The desire to rectify that loss and to provide an alternative that plugs this gap and plays the same global, anchoring role can, in such instances, be overwhelming. Indeed, it is precisely this reactive desire that might lead us to believe that moving beyond the anthropological difference will entail the adoption of a *single* alternative ontological and theoretical framework for illuminating the sense of the world and human and more-than-human-relations.

In view of these reactionary risks and temptations, one of the most striking and inspiring features of the present philosophical and theoretical scene is the veritable explosion of affirmative ontological frameworks aimed at rethinking the status of the animal and more-than-human worlds. Ontologies ranging from actor-network theories and multispecies ethnographies to new materialisms and new animisms have burst onto the theoretical and political scene, issuing courageous and forceful challenges to the traditional dogmas of anthropocentrism and human exceptionalism. The attentive reader will undoubtedly have noticed that my argument has made several points of explicit and implicit contact along the way with these and other non-anthropocentric ontological frameworks, which would seem to imply a commitment to a number of competing and sometimes conflicting ontological frameworks. What to make of this eclecticism? Is such profligacy at the ontological level simply the result of a lack of philosophical rigor, or are there deeper reasons for engaging with a variety of ontological approaches?

In closing, I wish to suggest that the multiplication of ontological frameworks in an affirmatively post-anthropocentric context is to be both expected and welcomed. On the one hand, we should expect plural ontologies in this context because of the scope and richness of the domains under consideration. The animal and more-than-human worlds can be conceptualized and encountered at a variety of levels and within innumerable registers of relation. Thus, we ought not to expect any single framework to exhaust this terrain or to provide exclusive coordinates for thought and practice. On the other hand, we should welcome the multiplication of post-anthropocentric ontological frameworks as a joyful *affirmation* of the extravagant, overflowing richness of planetary and cosmic life. Following Nietzsche, we might come to see the affirmation of plural ontologies as a way to avoid divesting "existence of its *rich ambiguity*," as a way to think and live with "good taste" and with "reverence for everything that lies beyond [our] horizon" (Nietzsche, 1974: 335). From this perspective, plural ontologies should be taken into consideration not out of a lack of theoretical rigor but rather as a means of experimenting, engaging, and creating with an inexhaustibly rich world. In surveying the wide variety of post-anthropocentric ontological frameworks on offer, our aim should not in the first instance be discerning which single framework best describes the basic "furniture" of the domains under consideration, but rather seeing what becomes possible for thought and life when a given framework is inhabited.

Readers with monistic ontological predilections (which is to say, readers who understand reality to be made of one kind of "stuff") might see such a stance as being relativistic and as encouraging the idea that any ontological framework is effectively as good as any other. However, in examining ontological approaches in the post-anthropocentric context in which we find ourselves, there are, in fact, various constraints and considerations that render some frameworks more attractive and more compelling than others – which is to say, not every ontology will be as good, helpful, illuminating, or persuasive as every other. First, it is important to recall that we have arrived on this post-anthropocentric ontological terrain as a way of trying to do justice to the complexities found specifically along the human/animal border, complexities that undo traditional claims concerning the anthropological difference and human uniqueness. Thus, the development of ontological perspectives that pay particular attention to this ontological region – and do so in ways that help disclose previously overlooked realities within this region – will be most salient to the task at hand of trying to develop a way of thinking that goes beyond the anthropological difference.

Another consideration to bear in mind when negotiating among the wide variety of non-anthropocentric ontologies presently on offer has to do with the deep ethological form of life outlined in Section 6. From a deep ethological perspective, ontologies can no longer be seen (as traditional approaches to ontology would have it) as an attempt to arrive at *the* correct human interpretation of the basic structure of the world – and not simply because of the ethnographic insight that ontologies often differ in profound ways across human cultures. The recent "ontological turn" in anthropology, which highlights the radical plurality of ontologies among human cultures, argues for viewing culturally-variant ontologies not simply as objects of intellectual curiosity for social scientists but as forms of thought that have autonomous importance and integrity. This anthropological commitment to ontological diversity leads to the position that there are many cultures and many natures (for human beings, at least) and that there should be no single, hegemonic ontological framework brought critically to bear on the worldviews and ontologies of other cultures.[37]

Beyond this anthropological stance, a deep ethological perspective leads us to a somewhat different conclusion concerning ontology – namely, that what we might call "human-formed" ontologies are themselves always already constituted with and through animals and more-than-human others. We always learn to see, make sense of, categorize, organize, engage, and experiment with the help of animals and more-than-human others of various sorts. Consequently, we cannot characterize ontologies solely as human or cultural constructs; ontologies are co-constituted in deep and fundamental ways in our ongoing entanglements with animals and various more-than-human others. To practice a deep ethological form of life is to commit to a continual revision and

---

[37] Holbraad and Pedersen (2017) provide a helpful overview of this work.

multiplication of ontological perspectives as we learn to inhabit more charitably and more respectfully the worlds and schemas not just of other "human" groups but those of more-than-human others as well. This practice of *syn-theōria*, of seeing-with others who are both human and more-than-human, brings ontology back to its practical calling; it also aligns – and even identifies – the task of doing ontology with living well. In other words, practicing ontology as a form of *syn-theōria* is the underlying normative ideal that animates the move beyond the anthropological difference. To practice ontology as a form of *syn-theōria* is, in effect, a way of enacting and experiencing some of the most profound forms of joy and flourishing with and between human, animal, and more-than-human worlds.[38]

With these constraints, considerations, and ideals in mind, we can then ask: Where do we find the richest, most sustained reflections on ontologies and ways of living that do justice to this kind of deep ethico-ethological vision? Although there are innumerable resources for such a project within Western intellectual and scientific traditions (some of which I have examined in the foregoing analysis), it is also crucial to recognize the deep debt that is owed here to non-Western cultures and to indigenous cultures in particular. Zoe Todd (2016) has aptly argued that many of the non-anthropocentric ontologies mentioned at the outset of this section have striking (and often unacknowledged) antecedents in indigenous ontologies, worldviews, and cosmologies. It is insufficient, however, simply to mark this overlap; what is needed on the part of those of us who wish to think about animals in a more affirmative and respectful way is a sustained and humble engagement with these often neglected intellectual and practical traditions. As Kim TallBear (2011) notes, efforts to reconfigure human-animal relationships on the basis of a more generous and respectful ontology of animals have longstanding precedents in both her own Lakota/Dakota tribal background and in related indigenous traditions.[39] Further, as TallBear also emphasizes, an engagement with indigenous worldviews can assist those of us who labor in the field of animal studies to think more carefully about what it means to embrace a broader set of relations beyond the scope of human-animal and animal-animal relations (see Section 7 for further discussion of this issue). Although it is no doubt essential to track the specific history of the

---

[38] For further observations on the importance of these alternative ethical affects, see Deborah Slicer's beautiful essay on cultivating more joy in human-animal relations (Slicer 2015).

[39] There is now a fairly rich literature exploring connections and tensions between animal studies, decolonial theory, and indigenous ontologies and forms of life. For important examples of such work, see Belcourt (2015), Deckha (2018), Fisher (2011), Hudson (2015), Robinson (2013), Singh (2018), and Womack (2013). My own thinking about these intersections has been shaped in profound ways by the fiction and non-fiction writings of Linda Hogan; see, especially, Hogan (1998).

subjugation of animals and to create new modes of relation in view of animals in particular, animal studies must also work to situate itself within a broader set of practices aimed at rethinking interactions with the entire (living *and* non-living) more-than-human world – or what many indigenous peoples refer to as "all our relations."[40] There are, to be sure, incommensurabilities between the kind of pro-animal work envisioned here and the recent theory and activism developed by resurgent indigenous and decolonial movements.[41] Yet, the contested intersection of animal studies with these and related projects aimed at the co-flourishing of human, animal, and more-than-human worlds provides the kind of fertile ground necessary for creating novel ways of thinking about and inhabiting our world as it continues to undergo unprecedented transformations.

---

[40] I have already mentioned Robinson's work (2013, 2014) in relation to this concept. See also King (1990) and LaDuke (1999) for further considerations.

[41] See Tuck and Yang (2012) for helpful ideas about incommensurabilities between decolonial projects and other justice struggles.

References

Adams, Carol J. (2015). *The Sexual Politics of Meat: A Feminist-Vegetarian Critical Theory*. New York: Bloomsbury.

Adams, Carol J. and Gruen, Lori (eds.) (2014). *Ecofeminism: Feminist Intersections with Other Animals and the Earth*. New York: Bloomsbury.

Aelian (1997). *Historical Miscellany*, N. G. Wilson, trans. Cambridge, MA: Harvard University Press.

Agamben, Giorgio (2004). *The Open: Man and Animal*, Kevin Attell, trans. Stanford, CA: Stanford University Press.

Alexandratos, Nikos and Bruinsma, Jelle (2012). *World Agriculture towards 2030/2050: The 2012 Revision*. Rome: FAO.

Asdal, Kristin, Druglitrö, Tone, and Hinchliffe, Steve (eds.) (2017). *Humans, Animals, and Biopolitics: The More-than-Human Condition*. London: Routledge.

Bard, Kim A. and Leavens, David A. (2014). The Importance of Development for Comparative Primatology. *Annual Review of Anthropology*, 43, 183–200.

Belcourt, Billy-Ray (2015). Animal Bodies, Colonial Subjects: (Re)Locating Animality in Decolonial Thought. *Societies*, 5: 1–11.

Best, Steven (2014). *The Politics of Total Liberation: Revolution for the 21st Century*. New York: Palgrave Macmillan.

Boisseron, Bénédicte (2018). *Afro-Dog: Blackness and the Animal Question*. New York: Columbia University Press.

Braidotti, Rosi (2013). *The Posthuman*. Cambridge: Polity Press.

Calarco, Matthew (2008). *Zoographies: The Question of the Animal from Heidegger to Derrida*. New York: Columbia University Press.

Calarco, Matthew (2014). Being toward Meat: Anthropocentrism, Indistinction, and Veganism. *Dialectical Anthropology*, 38: 415–29.

Calarco, Matthew (2015). *Thinking through Animals: Identity, Difference, Indistinction*. Stanford, CA: Stanford University Press.

Calarco, Matthew (2018). The Three Ethologies. In Dominik Ohrem and Matthew Calarco, eds., *Exploring Animal Encounters: Philosophical, Cultural, and Historical Perspectives*. Switzerland: Palgrave Macmillan.

Campbell, Gordon Lindsay (ed.) (2014). *The Oxford Handbook of Animals in Classical Thought and Life*. New York: Oxford University Press.

Chen, Mel Y. (2012). *Animacies: Biopolitics, Racial Mattering, and Queer Affect*. Durham, NC: Duke University Press.

Clark, Emily (2012). "The Animal" and "The Feminist". *Hypatia*, 27: 516–20.

Collins, Patricia Hill and Bilge, Sirma (2016). *Intersectionality*. Malden, MA: Polity Press.

Crist, Eileen (2018). Anthropocentrism. In Noel Castree, Mike Hulme, and James D. Proctor, eds., *Companion to Environmental Studies*. New York: Routledge.

de Waal, Frans (2016). *Are We Smart Enough to Know How Smart Animals Are?* New York: W.W. Norton.

Deckha, Maneesha (2018). Postcolonial. In Lori Gruen, ed., *Critical Terms for Animal Studies*. Chicago: University of Chicago Press.

Deleuze, Gilles (1988). *Spinoza: Practical Philosophy*, Robert Hurley, trans. San Francisco: City Lights Books.

Derrida, Jacques (2008). *The Animal That Therefore I Am*, David Wills, trans. New York: Fordham University Press.

Derrida, Jacques and Roudinesco, Elisabeth (2004). *For What Tomorrow . . .: A Dialogue*, Jeff Fort, trans. Stanford, CA: Stanford University Press.

Despret, Vinciane (2016). *What Would Animals Say If We Asked the Right Questions?* Brett Buchanan, trans. Minneapolis: University of Minnesota Press.

Donovan, Josephine and Adams, Carol J. (eds.) (1996). *Beyond Animal Rights: A Feminist Caring Ethic for the Treatment of Animals*. New York: Continuum.

Enard, Wolfgang, Przeworski, Molly, Fisher, Simon E. et al. (2002). Molecular Evolution of FOXP2, a Gene Involved in Speech and Language. *Nature*, 418: 869–72.

Esposito, Roberto (2012). *Third Person: Politics of Life and Philosophy of the Impersonal*, Zakiya Hanafi, trans. Cambridge: Polity Press.

Fisher, Linda (2011). Freeing Feathered Spirits. In Lisa A. Kemmerer, ed., *Sister Species: Women, Animals and Social Justice*. Urbana: University of Illinois Press.

Food and Agriculture Organization of the United Nations (2014). *Food Outlook: Biannual Report on Global Food Markets*. Rome: FAO.

Foucault, Michel (2011). *The Courage of Truth: The Government of Self and Others II, Lectures at the Collège de France 1983–1984*, Graham Burchell, trans. New York: Palgrave Macmillan.

Glock, Hans-Johann (2012). The Anthropological Difference: What Can Philosophers Do to Identify the Differences between Human and Non-human Animals? *Royal Institute of Philosophy Supplement*, 70: 105–31.

Grusin, Richard (ed.) (2015). *The Nonhuman Turn*. Minneapolis: University of Minnesota Press.

Guattari, Félix (2000). *The Three Ecologies*, Ian Pindar and Paul Sutton, trans. London: Athlone Press.

Haraway, Donna J. (2003). *Companion Species Manifesto.* Chicago: Prickly Paradigm Press.

Haraway, Donna J. (2008). *When Species Meet.* Minneapolis: University of Minnesota Press.

Harper, A. Breeze (ed.) (2010). *Sistah Vegan: Black Female Vegans Speak on Food, Identity, Health, and Society.* Brooklyn, NY: Lantern Books.

Heath, John (2005). *The Talking Greeks: Speech, Animals, and the Other in Homer, Aeschylus, and Plato.* New York: Cambridge University Press.

Hogan, Linda (1998a). First People. In Linda Hogan, Deena Metzger, and Brenda Peterson, eds., *Intimate Nature: The Bond between Women and Animals.* New York: Fawcett.

Holbraad, Martin and Pedersen, Morten A. (2017). *The Ontological Turn: An Anthropological Exposition.* Cambridge: Cambridge University Press.

Hu, Hai Yang, He, Liu, Fominykh, Kseniya, et al. (2012). Evolution of the Human-Specific microRNA miR-941. *Nature Communications,* 3 (2012): 1145.

Hudson, Brian K. (2015). A Seat at the Table: Political Representation for Animals. In Deborah L. Madsen, ed. *The Routledge Companion to Native American Literature,* New York: Routledge.

Hull, David L. (1989). *The Metaphysics of Evolution.* Albany: State University of New York Press.

Hutto, Joe (2014a). *Touching the Wild: Living with the Mule Deer of Deadman Gulch.* New York: Skyhorse Publishing.

Hutto, Joe (2014b). *Touching the Wild: Living with the Mule Deer of Deadman Gulch,* DVD, David Allen, dir. Alexandria, VA: PBS Home Video.

Jones, Dena and Pawlinger, Michelle (2017). Voluntary Standards and their Impact on National Laws and International Initiatives. In Gabriela Steier and Kiran K. Patel, eds., *International Farm Animal, Wildlife and Food Safety Law.* Switzerland: Springer International Publishing.

Kim, Claire Jean (2015). *Dangerous Crossings: Race, Species, and Nature in a Multicultural Age.* New York: Cambridge University Press.

King, Thomas (1990). Introduction. In Thomas King, ed., *All My Relations: An Anthology of Contemporary Canadian Fiction.* Toronto: McClelland and Stewart.

Kronfeldner, Maria, Roughley, Neil, and Toepfer, Georg (2014). Recent Work on Human Nature: Beyond Traditional Essences. *Philosophy Compass,* 9: 642–52.

LaDuke, Winona (1999). *All Our Relations: Native Struggles for Land and Life.* Chicago: Haymarket Books.

Laertius, Diogenes (2018). *Lives of the Eminent Philosophers,* Pamela Mensch, trans. Oxford: Oxford University Press.

Laland, Kevin N. and Galef, Bennett G. (eds.) (2009). *The Question of Animal Culture*. Cambridge, MA: Harvard University Press.

Lents, Nathan (2016). *Not So Different: Finding Human Nature in Animals*. New York: Columbia University Press.

Leopold, Aldo (1989). *A Sand County Almanac, and Sketches Here and There*. New York: Oxford University Press.

Lorimer, Jamie (2015). *Wildlife in the Anthropocene: Conservation after Nature*. Minneapolis: University of Minnesota Press.

Massumi, Brian (2014). *What Animals Teach Us about Politics*. Durham, NC: Duke University Press.

McEvilley, Thomas (2002). *The Shape of Ancient Thought: Comparative Studies in Greek and Indian Philosophies*. New York: Allworth Press.

Newmyer, Stephen T. (2010). *Animals in Greek and Roman Thought: A Sourcebook*. New York: Routledge.

Nibert, David (2002). *Animal Rights/Human Rights: Entanglements of Oppression and Liberation*. Lanham, MD: Rowman & Littlefield.

Nietzsche, Friedrich (1967). *The Will to Power*, Walter Kaufmann and R. J. Hollingdale, trans. New York: Vintage Books.

Nietzsche, Friedrich (1974). *The Gay Science: With a Prelude in Rhymes and an Appendix of Songs*, Walter Kaufmann, trans. New York: Vintage Books.

Nocella II, Anthony J., Bentley, Judy K. C., and Duncan, Janet M. (eds.) (2012). *Earth, Animal, and Disability Liberation: The Rise of the Eco-ability Movement*. New York: Peter Lang.

Pellow, David N. (2014). *Total Liberation: The Power and Promise of Animal Rights and the Radical Earth Movement*. Minneapolis: University of Minnesota Press.

Plumwood, Val (2002). *Environmental Culture: The Ecological Crisis of Reason*. New York: Routledge.

Puar, Jasbir (2011). "I Would Rather Be a Cyborg Than a Goddess": Intersectionality, Assemblage, and Affective Politics. *Transversal* (2), http://eipcp.net/transversal/0811/puar/en

Pugliese, Joseph (2013). *State Violence and the Execution of Law: Biopolitical Caesurae of Torture, Black Sites, Drones*. New York: Routledge.

Rachels, James (1991). *Created from Animals: The Moral Implications of Darwinism*. New York: Oxford University Press.

Robinson, Margaret (2013). Veganism and Mi'kmaq Legends. *Canadian Journal of Native Studies*, 33: 189–96.

Robinson, Margaret (2014). Aboriginal Veganism, www.youtube.com/watch?v=8t2mK92H63E

Ryder, Richard (1989). *Animal Revolution: Changing Attitudes towards Speciesism*. Oxford: Basil Blackwell.

Ryder, Richard (1998). Speciesism. In Marc Bekoff and Carron A. Meaney, eds., *Encyclopedia of Animal Rights and Animal Welfare*. Westport, CT: Greenwood Press.

Seiler, Andreas and Helldin, J.-O. (2006). Mortality in Wildlife Due to Transportation. In John Davenport and Julia L. Davenport, eds., *The Ecology of Transportation: Managing Mobility for the Environment*. New York: Springer.

Singer, Peter (2002). *Animal Liberation*. New York: Ecco.

Singer, Peter (2009). Foreword. In Paola Cavalieri, ed., *The Death of the Animal: A Dialogue*. New York: Columbia University Press.

Singh, Julietta (2018). *Unthinking Mastery: Dehumanism and Decolonial Entanglements*. Durham, NC: Duke University Press.

Slicer, Deborah (2015). More Joy. *Ethics and the Environment*, 20: 1–23.

Socha, Kim (2013). The "Dreaded Comparisons" and Speciesism: Leveling the Hierarchy of Suffering. In Kim Socha and Sarahjane Blum, eds., *Confronting Animal Exploitation: Grassroots Essays on Liberation and Veganism*. Jefferson, NC: McFarland.

Spiegel, Marjorie (1996). *The Dreaded Comparison: Human and Animal Slavery*. New York: Mirror Books.

Stanescu, James K. (2013). Beyond Biopolitics: Animal Studies, Factory Farms, and the Advent of Deading Life. *PhaenEx*, 8: 135–60.

Steffen, Will, Richardson, Katherine, Rockström, Johan et al. (2015). Planetary Boundaries: Guiding Human Development on a Changing Planet. *Science*, 347: 736–46.

Steiner, Gary (2005). *Anthropocentrism and Its Discontents: The Moral Status of Animals in the History of Western Philosophy*. Pittsburgh, PA: University of Pittsburgh Press.

TallBear, Kim (2011). Why Interspecies Thinking Needs Indigenous Standpoints. *Fieldsights – Theorizing the Contemporary, Cultural Anthropology Online*, http://culanth.org/fieldsights/260-why-interspecies-thinking-needs-indigenous-standpoints

Taylor, Sunaura (2017). *Beasts of Burden: Animal and Disability Liberation*. New York: New Press.

Todd, Zoe (2016). An Indigenous Feminist's Take on the Ontological Turn: "Ontology" Is Just Another Word for Colonialism. *Journal of Historical Sociology*, 29: 4–22.

Tuck, Eve and Yang, K. Wayne (2012). Decolonization Is Not a Metaphor. *Decolonization: Indigeneity, Education & Society*, 1: 1–40.

Tyler, Tom (2009). If Horses Had Hands . . .. In Tom Tyler and Manuela Rossini, eds., *Animal Encounters*. Boston: Brill.

van Dooren, Thom (2018). Extinction. In Lori Gruen, ed., *Critical Terms for Animal Studies*. Chicago: University of Chicago Press.

Virgil (1963). *The Eclogues; The Georgics*, C. Day Lewis, trans. Oxford: Oxford University Press.

Wadiwel, Dinesh J. (2015). *The War against Animals*. Leiden: Brill.

Wolch, Jennifer (1998). Zoopolis. In Jennifer Wolch and Jody Emel, eds., *Animal Geographies: Places, Politics, and Identity in the Nature-Culture Borderlands*. London: Verso.

Wolfe, Cary (2013). *Before the Law: Humans and Other Animals in a Biopolitical Frame*. Chicago: University of Chicago Press.

Womack, Craig (2013). There is No Respectful Way to Kill an Animal. *Studies in American Indian Literatures*, 25: 11–27.

World Wildlife Fund (2014). *Living Planet Report 2014: Species and Spaces, People and Places*. Gland, Switzerland: World Wildlife Fund.

Wright, Kate (2017). *Transdisciplinary Journeys in the Anthropocene: More-than-Human Encounters*. New York: Routledge.

Acknowledgments

I am thankful, first and foremost, to Christina and Luce for their patience, love, and support during the writing process. I am grateful also to the many colleagues and students with whom I have discussed the ideas presented here over the past few years. This project has benefited enormously from feedback from the series editors and anonymous reviewers for the press; I am grateful for the time they have taken to engage my work. I dedicate this book to my parents, who have taught me through their words and actions what it means to care for our animal relations.

Permissions

An earlier version of parts of Section 1 appeared in "Genealogies," in Lynn Turner, Ron Broglio, Undine Sellbach, eds., *The Edinburgh Companion to Animal Studies*, Edinburgh University Press, 2018. This material is used here, in modified form, with the permission of Edinburgh University Press through PLSclear, which I gratefully acknowledge. An earlier version of parts of Section 2 appeared in "Revisiting the Anthropological Difference," in Serpil Oppermann and Serenella Iovino, eds., *Environmental Humanities: Voices from the Anthropocene*, Rowman & Littlefield, 2016. This material is used here, in modified form, with the permission of Rowman & Littlefield, which I gratefully acknowledge. An earlier version of parts of Section 3 appeared in "Reorienting Strategies for Animal Justice," in Paola Cavalieri, ed., *Philosophy and the Politics of Animal Liberation*, Palgrave Macmillan, 2016. This material is used here, in modified form, with the permission of Palgrave Macmillan, which I gratefully acknowledge.

Cambridge Elements ☰

Environmental Humanities

Louise Westling
University of Oregon

Louise Westling is an American scholar of literature and environmental humanities who was a founding member of the Association for the Study of Literature and Environment and its President in 1998. She has been active in the international movement for environmental cultural studies, teaching and writing on landscape imagery in literature, critical animal studies, biosemiotics, phenomenology, and deep history.

Serenella Iovino
University of North Carolina at Chapel Hill

Serenella Iovino is Professor of Italian Studies and Environmental Humanities at the University of North Carolina at Chapel Hill. She has written on a wide range of topics, including environmental ethics and ecocritical theory, bioregionalism and landscape studies, ecofeminism and posthumanism, comparative literature, eco-art, and the Anthropocene.

Timo Maran
University of Tartu

Timo Maran is an Estonian semiotician and poet. Maran is Professor of Ecosemiotics and Environmental Humanities and Head of the Department of Semiotics at the University of Tartu. His research interests are semiotic relations of nature and culture, Estonian nature writing, zoosemiotics and species conservation, semiotics of biological mimicry.

About the Series

The environmental humanities is a new transdisciplinary complex of approaches to the embeddedness of human life and culture in all the dynamics that characterize the life of the planet. These approaches reexamine our species' history in light of the intensifying awareness of drastic climate change and ongoing mass extinction. To engage this reality, Cambridge Elements in Environmental Humanities builds on the idea of a more hybrid and participatory mode of research and debate, connecting critical and creative fields.

Cambridge Elements ☰

Environmental Humanities

Elements in the Series

The Anatomy of Deep Time: Rock Art and Landscape in the Altai
Mountains of Mongolia
Esther Jacobson-Tepfer

Beyond the Anthropological Difference
Matthew Calarco

A full series listing is available at: www.cambridge.org/EIEH